W9-BKA-490

WRITE
TO THE
POINT!

Letters, Memos,
and Reports
That Get Results

Rosemary T. Fruehling
and N. B. Oldham

McGRAW-HILL BOOK COMPANY
New York   St. Louis   San Francisco
Hamburg   Mexico   Toronto

Copyright © 1988 by Rosemary Fruehling and N. B. Oldham. All rights reserved. Printed in the United States of America. Except as permitted under the Copyright Act of 1976, no part of this publication may be reproduced or distributed in any form or by any means or stored in a data base or retrieval system without the prior written permission of the publisher.

2 3 4 5 6 7 8 9 DOC DOC 8 9 2 1 0 9

ISBN 0-07-022549-4

Library of Congress Cataloging-in-Publication Data

Fruehling, Rosemary T., 1933–
Write to the point!

Includes index.
  1. Letter-writing. 2. Report writing.
3. English language—Rhetoric.   I. Oldham, N. B.
II. Title.
PE1483.F73 1986   808'.042   86-10288
ISBN 0-07-022549-4

Book design by Eve Kirch

CONTENTS

INTRODUCTION: WHY WRITE TO THE POINT?   1

    A FAST PACE   2
    HEAVY COMPETITION FOR ATTENTION   2
    WRITTEN WORDS MUST ACT ALONE   3
    THE APPROACH   3

Section One. EFFECTIVE WRITING SKILLS 5

1.   WRITING HABITS: THE BASE   7

    INVOLVE THE RECEIVER   7
    FOUR BAD WRITING HABITS   8
    FOUR GOOD WRITING HABITS   13
    SUMMING UP   23

2.   WRITE WITH STYLE   24

    THE CARING TONE   25
    MORE ABOUT TONE   26
    GETTING THINGS DONE   27
    THE READER'S INTEREST   32
    THE YOU ATTITUDE   35
    MORE ABOUT YOU AND I   39

THE VOICE OF AUTHORITY   40
BE POSITIVE AND DIRECT   42
I'M THE ONE FOR YOU   44
STANDING OUT FROM THE CROWD   47
HUMOR, SARCASM, ANGER: BEWARE   48
SUMMING UP   49

3. PUTTING WORDS IN THEIR PLACE   50

TAKE GRAMMAR EASILY   50
SENTENCES   51
PARAGRAPHS   56
SUMMING UP   63

4. PUNCTUATION, SPELLING, LEGIBILITY   65

THAT PESKY PUNCTUATION   65
SPELLING MATTERS   74
LEGIBILITY   79
SUMMING UP   81

Section Two. LETTER ELEMENTS   83

5. LETTER ELEMENTS AND FORMATS   85

RETURN ADDRESS (LETTERHEAD)   85
DATE   89
INTERIOR ADDRESS   91
ATTENTION LINE (B)   93
SALUTATION   93
SUBJECT LINE (B)   100
BODY   101
COMPLIMENTARY CLOSE   101
NAME AND SIGNATURE   105
REFERENCE INITIALS (B)   106
ENCLOSURES (B)   106
COPY NOTATIONS (B)   107
POSTSCRIPT   108
BUSINESS LETTER FORMATS   109
SUMMING UP   114

Section Three. EFFECTIVE WRITING AT WORK   115

6. TYPICAL BUSINESS LETTERS   117

    PROVIDING INFORMATION   118
    SEEKING INFORMATION   120
    SELLING: PLEASANT PERSUASION   122
    BUSINESS LETTER OF INTRODUCTION   126
    MAKING A RESERVATION   127
    CONFIRMING A RESERVATION   128
    ASKING   128
    AGREEING   131
    DECLINING   132
    OFFERING CREDIT: GOOD NEWS   133
    REFUSING CREDIT: BAD NEWS   134
    SEEKING PAYMENT: UNPLEASANT PERSUASION   135
    OFFERING A JOB: GOOD NEWS   137
    REJECTING A JOB APPLICANT: BAD NEWS   139
    RESIGNING   140
    SUMMING UP   142

7. EFFECTIVE MEMOS   143

    THE CYA SYNDROME   144
    MEMOS ARE NECESSARY   144
    STANDARD HEADINGS   144
    30-SECOND MEMOS   146
    MEMO ETIQUETTE   146
    CATEGORICAL SAMPLES   147
    SUMMING UP   163

8. REPORTS   165

    AN OUTLINE—THE FIRST STEP   166
    RESEARCH IS VITAL   166
    GOOD NOTES = GOOD REPORTS   167
    BASIC ELEMENTS   168
    OPTIONAL ELEMENTS   173
    SUMMING UP   176

Section Four. EFFECTIVE WRITING AT HOME 177

9. WRITING FOR PLEASURE 179

WRITING TO FRIENDS 180
COMMUNAL LETTERS 183
CONGRATULATIONS 185
THANK YOU 186
INVITATIONS 188
ACCEPTING OR DECLINING 190
INTRODUCING 191
REFERENCES 192
CONDOLENCES 195
SUMMING UP 196

10. WRITING FOR ACTION 198

REQUESTING CREDIT 198
"I CAN'T PAY" LETTERS 201
CREDIT CARD LETTERS 201
LETTERS SEEKING INFORMATION 203
LETTERS OF COMPLAINT 204
PLACING ORDERS 208
WRITING TO CONGRESS 209
LETTERS TO THE EDITOR 212
COLLEGE APPLICATION ESSAYS 216
MINUTES OF THE MEETING 220
SUMMING UP 222

11. WRITING FOR A JOB 223

RÉSUMÉ 223
COVER LETTER 237
FISHING LETTER 240
REFERENCE REQUEST LETTER 242
FOLLOW-UP LETTER 244
ACCEPTING A JOB OFFER 246
DECLINING A JOB OFFER 247
SUMMING UP 248

A FINAL WORD 249

USEFUL REFERENCE WORKS 250

INDEX 253

Introduction:
Why Write to the Point?

To exist in our society, you must communicate. You communicate every day to get and give information, to seek and give help, to control and direct others. You communicate to function effectively. Most of the time you communicate face-to-face by talking, which is the *oral* form of *verbal* communication (using words), and by gesturing, which is *nonverbal* communication.

You carry out all this oral and nonverbal face-to-face communication matter-of-factly. Communicating is a part of your life, and you do it daily, constantly, almost without thought. Some do it better than others, some do it more often than others, but all communicate.

Often you must communicate when you cannot be face-to-face or use the telephone. Then you must resort to *writing*—another form of verbal communication. Most of this writing is in the form of letters, business and personal. People in business also need to write memoranda (memos), reports, project proposals, agendas, and minutes of meetings.

Many people who have no trouble getting their point across when speaking have nothing but trouble when writing. You can do many things in face-to-face communication—shout, wave a fist, smile, grab the other person—to command attention and get your point across. You can also see immediately whether your message is being understood and take steps to make sure that it is. When writing, you cannot do any of these things to convey your message. The words you write must convey your meaning—and they must do it quickly!

1

A FAST PACE

If your written message requires more than a minute of your reader's time to make its point, your reader is unlikely to get to that point or to care much upon finally grasping it. Write to the point. Our society moves at a fast pace. People are conditioned by 30-second television commercials to expect the whole message in a short time. To communicate successfully in writing, craft your message so that it takes no more than a minute to read.

The average person can read 260 to 300 words in a minute, which is about one page of double-spaced typing. If your message requires more words, it may well fail to come across. Most business or nonpersonal letters should convey their messages so that receivers can read them in 30 seconds!

If you doubt much information can be conveyed in 30 seconds, take a look at one of those 30-second television spots. Those spots, of course, rely on both the spoken word and dramatic pictures to convey their messages; when writing, you have only the words you write to do the job. Don't worry—with a little thought and effort, and the writing skills and tips in this book, you will write to the point and create effective messages.

HEAVY COMPETITION FOR ATTENTION

In addition to having to grab a reader's attention in a little time, your writing faces heavy competition for that attention. Thousands of written ideas and messages surround us. Think of all that junk mail stuffed into your mailbox each day. Signals and messages constantly bombard everyone, including the person you want to reach.

You must propel your written message through all that flak to your target. You cannot shout or grab the lapels of your receiver to command attention—but you can use the great power of the written word to grab your receiver by the lapels figuratively. You can make your written words cut through all those other signals, get the attention of your reader, and drive your message home. You can do this by using the right words in the right place to write to the point. This book will help you—whatever kind of writing you do.

WRITTEN WORDS MUST ACT ALONE

Before you read about some of the specific skills needed to craft a 1-minute message, consider these general guidelines about the written word. Unlike your spoken words, which you can reinforce in so many ways, your written words must do the job by themselves. Used effectively, however, the written word can be a powerful tool, and it has advantages that the spoken word lacks:

- The written word can be precise.

- The written word is less likely to be misunderstood if used correctly.

- The written word is permanent and thus its effectiveness extends over time.

Ironically, the potential advantages of the written word increase the pressure on you as a writer. Whereas a mistaken or ineffectual spoken word can be easily and immediately adjusted ("Oh, I didn't mean that." "I didn't say that." "This is what I really meant to say.") and vanishes quickly into the air, an equivalent written slip has lasting consequences, which you are not present to correct or explain.

THE APPROACH

As you go through this book, you will learn the basics necessary in all writing, from spelling and punctuation to style and attitude. These will help whether you are writing for a motel reservation or the great American novel. You will learn the fundamental elements of any good letter and the formatting options that give your message the feel you desire, whether formal and old-fashioned or breezy and modern.

You will discover the nitty-gritty of business letter writing, the decisions and details that help ensure an enthusiastic reception of your message. This book takes a unique approach to the "rules" of good writing. It examines specific examples, both good and bad, and derives general concepts from them. This approach reflects the natural way you develop language skills: you didn't learn grammar before you learned how to talk! The book presents authentic cases to show what works and what doesn't, what concepts apply across the board, and how you can use these concepts to perfect your writing.

The book uses mostly good examples that you can safely adapt for your own use. Be aware, though, that both good and *bad* examples are used. Don't pick up a bad example to use. (The bad ones will be marked.) Study the bad examples to avoid their mistakes. They are included to instruct you, for as Montaigne suggested, we can learn more readily from bad examples than from good ones: "There may be some people of my temperament, who learn better by contrast than by example...a bad way of speaking reforms mine better than a good one."

Finally, you will delve into the practical side of writing at home, with examples of résumés, job-seeking letters, complaints, credit requests, and a host of other important messages. The inductive approach continues, and you will learn how to improve your pleasurable writing as well—letters to friends and relatives, thank-you notes, invitations, and so on.

It is not necessary to read the book straight through from beginning to end to benefit from it. Look in the table of contents for what you need and concentrate on that. A complete reading will, however, be beneficial.

When you finish, you will be prepared to put the writing ideas to work for yourself. You will have seen how a little concentration and a few simple concepts can help make everything you write "to the point."

SECTION ONE

EFFECTIVE WRITING SKILLS

This section gives you the basics necessary to any effective writing, whether at home or in the office, for business or for pleasure, to one person or to many. Chapter 1 identifies four bad writing habits that may sabotage your efforts, and introduces four good habits that can help you write to the point.

Chapter 2, using an inductive approach, shows you what style is all about. You will discover writing rules as practical applications, rather than as abstractions imposed from above. Chapter 3 will help you put words in their place—a painless path to grammar basics.

Chapter 4 provides a commonsense approach to spelling, punctuation, and legibility—the raw materials that you use in any writing.

Writing Habits: The Base

We write to communicate.

Such an obvious statement hardly needs to be made—or so it would seem. A lot of people, however, do *not* communicate when they write. They *mis*communicate.

Why? Because writing effectively to communicate does demand some thought and a bit of practice—nothing more than the average person can muster. Writing—the everyday, essential writing that is our topic—is not an obscure, esoteric skill that only a few can master.

Despite what your school experience may have led you to believe, rules of writing rest on common sense. They help communication. Punctuation, for example, is nothing more than an attempt to do in writing what we do with gestures, a change of voice, or pauses, when speaking.

If we miscommunicate when writing, it is not because the mechanics of writing are too difficult to master. To paraphrase Shakespeare, the fault is not in the rules of writing, but in ourselves.

INVOLVE THE RECEIVER

Because the written word can pack more power than the spoken word, written communication requires more thought and planning.

The more thought and planning you invest, the more likely you will write to the point.

As in all communication, writing involves the sender (you the writer) and the receiver. Since receivers are not in front of you when you write, you must make an effort to involve them. You should:

- Develop a mental image of the receivers
- Imagine what would attract the attention of the receivers
- Decide exactly what message you wish to convey

Your job as a writer is to develop the right ideas and find the right words to grab the attention of the *specific* person with whom you want to communicate. In other words,

COMMUNICATION IS THE PROCESS OF INVOLVING,

and involving your reader is the first step toward writing to the point.

FOUR BAD WRITING HABITS

The misplaced comma or the misspelled word will not help your written communication, but written miscommunication more often results from four bad writing habits. We *hedge,* we *use too many words,* we *use big words,* and we *fake interest.* Collectively and individually, these bad habits can sabotage your point.

Hedging

We hedge when we do not express exactly and directly what we mean:

A Hedge   Due to unexpected and continued high usage of health care services covered under the Comprehensive Health Care Plan, it will be necessary to make a rate adjustment effective January 1, 199_ .

The Gist Our Comprehensive Health Care Plan rates will increase effective January 1, 199_ .

COMMENT: In the first version, the writer tries to soften the bad news, but only makes it worse. Since it does not say clearly that rates will be raised, an optimistic reader might be forgiven for thinking increased use means rates will actually go down.

A Hedge Your request for research funds has been thoroughly reviewed with great interest. Although it has much merit, it has been regretfully determined that a negative response must be given at this time.

The Gist We are sorry but, although your request has merit, we cannot grant the research funds.

COMMENT: In trying to let the applicant down easily, the first version may build false hopes that the request will be granted at a later time. If this is so, say so; otherwise, avoid suggesting it. A "no" is a "no," and trying to disguise it only confuses and angers. As the improved version shows, you can write a denial that is to the point and still sympathetic.

A Hedge In regard to your request for immediate payment, compliance is impeded by a temporary cash flow situation, which, it is hoped, will be rectified in the near future.

The Gist We cannot pay you right now but hope to be able to next month.

COMMENT: In the first version, the writer uses big words [see "Using Big Words," below] to disguise the fact that she or he will not be paying the bill. A direct statement and a specific time for making payment will make the message clear and persuasive.

A Hedge Information concerning your current rates for certificates of deposits would be helpful.

The Gist Please send me your current certificate of deposit rates.

COMMENT: The first version is simply unclear. Does the writer want information, or is he or she only expressing a polite interest? A busy reader might throw the letter away without taking any action.

TIP: Hedgers most often use the passive voice. See "Be Active," later in this chapter.

We hedge when we write because words fixed on a page deliver more impact than do words formed temporarily in the air. We fear sounding rude by being blunt, which, of course, we should not sound. But you can be direct without being rude. Hedging is rude.

Sometimes, as you will read, a hedge might be the best way to deliver an unwelcome message. But, in general, hedging clouds your message and blocks communication. Even if the message does manage to seep through, the hedge more often than not puts the reader off, which violates that fundamental principle of good writing to the point:

INVOLVE THE READER.

Using Too Many Words

Lack of confidence in our writing skill causes us to develop the bad habit of using too many words. In an effort to strengthen our message, we smother it, following the false logic of "if one word is good, two must be better."

Usually, fewer words will convey your message more effectively, and, of course, your reader need not struggle through a swamp of useless words to find your meaning. It is a struggle most readers will not make today.

Wordy   The company has on its payroll a total of 5684 employees, of which 1793 are in the salaried and 3891 in the hourly rated groups.

Succinct   The company has 5684 employees, of which 1793 are salaried and 3891 are hourly rated.

COMMENT: The unnecessary words are evident: "on its payroll a total," "in the," "in the" again, and "groups." All these words are *redundant*. They increase the reader's work while adding nothing to her or his understanding.

Wordy In this package I am returning the new sweater that I purchased from your store. The invoice number of my order is 3761.SW. I am returning this sweater because it is too small in size. This is size medium. I need a larger size. Please send me size large. Thank you.

Succinct I am returning this sweater because it is too small. Please send me size large. The invoice number is 3761.SW. Thank you.

COMMENT: The succinct version says it all with some 30 fewer words. Redundant words in the wordy version include "invoice number *of my order*," "too small *in size*." Many of the other words give unnecessary information. Obviously you are returning it in the package, and you purchased it from the store to which you return it. Also, if it is too small, you need not waste your or the reader's time saying you need a larger size.

When you write, try to avoid saying the same thing twice. Look for the redundant words and cut them out. The faster your reader gets the message, the faster you will get the action you desire.

Using Big Words

Many people find writing an imposing task, so they feel they must use big words. Other people just want to show off their knowledge of big words. When you cultivate the bad habit of using big or unfamiliar words, you do not aid communication. You and your writing just become *pompous*. It is not the big word, but the right word, that counts.

Pompous Indicate the direction toward my domicile. I am fatigued and I aspire to retire. I consumed a minuscule libation approximately sixty minutes hence, and it forthwith affected my cerebellum.

Plain   Show me the way to go home. I'm tired and I want to go to bed. I had a little drink about an hour ago, and it went straight to my head.

COMMENT: How many would recognize the straightforward old song in the pompous version? How many would want to bother singing it—or reading it?

Pompous   Your epistle arrived at a most felicitous moment.

Plain   Your letter arrived at a good time.

Pompous   Prices were impacted adversely by the season's aridity, which was deleterious to agriculture.

Plain   The dry season hurt the crops and caused prices to rise.

COMMENT: Select words to carry your message, not to dress up the page. Avoid the practice of the young lady in Wonderland of whom Lewis Carroll said, "Alice had not the slightest idea what Latitude was, or Longitude either, but she thought they were nice grand words to say." Write to express, not to impress.

Faking Interest

Often we try so hard to convince readers of our interest that we give the impression that we do not really feel what we are writing. Some of us develop this bad habit by overreacting to suggestions we should use fewer "I's" and more "you's." We overdo it and as a result open ourselves to suspicion of insincerity. That suspicion can stop our message getting through, as in the second example below.

Using too many superlatives ("most" words: *biggest, fastest, utmost, best;* also *splendid, outstanding, fantastic, great, wonderful, awesome*) will also make you appear hypocritical. Such words are overused in advertising and by gushy writers. Readers become conditioned to tune them out. Use them sparingly, if at all.

Fake   It is with the utmost sincerity that I extend to you felicitations on your recent, well-deserved promotion.

Genuine   Congratulations! You earned it.

COMMENT: The reader of the first version might sense a bit of envy behind the words, a message the writer did not intend. Notice also how the phrase "utmost sincerity" sounds terribly phony. Rather than *tell* the reader you are sincere, let it come out in the message itself.

Fake Your qualifications and experience are splendid, and we are sure that you will have no trouble finding a position equal to your outstanding talents, but we have hired another candidate who more closely matches our immediate needs to fill the position for which you applied. We sincerely appreciate your thinking of us and will keep your excellent résumé in our files.

Genuine Although your qualifications and experience are excellent, we have hired another person whose background more closely fits our needs. Thank you for applying, and good luck in your job search.

COMMENT: The writer of the first version might genuinely feel sorry for the person he or she had to turn down, but overwriting sends a message that drips insincerity.

Faking interest is the reverse of hedging—the faker is overanxious to get a message across as opposed to trying to avoid sending the message. But both reflect insincerity. Also, they amplify the other two bad writing habits: big words and too many words.

If you find that your message seems insincere but can't see how to change that, try cutting words and using simpler ones. You may find that the words you cut are the very ones that sounded insincere, particularly superlatives. They clutter up your message, destroy the sense of sincerity, and blunt your point. Remember to express genuine interest and concern for the reader without overdoing it.

FOUR GOOD WRITING HABITS

There are four good writing habits—corresponding to and counteracting the four bad writing habits—that make up the core of all effective writing. These good habits will help you write to the point by eliminating useless words and sharpening the useful ones.

Be Active

The habitual use of the active voice...makes for forcible writing. ...[W]hen a sentence is made stronger, it usually becomes shorter. Thus, brevity is a by-product of vigor.
(*The Elements of Style* by William Strunk, Jr., and E. B. White.)

You can write in the *passive voice* or the *active voice*. The passive voice is the voice of the hedger. It is weak and impersonal. The active voice is strong, direct, and clear. It is personal. You will sometimes want to use the passive voice, but as a rule,

WRITE IN THE ACTIVE VOICE.

In the passive voice, the subject of the sentence is acted upon. In the active voice, the subject of the sentence acts.

Study the following examples and note how the active voice delivers the message with more force.

Passive   Your letter of May 8, 1986, was received yesterday.

Active   Your letter of May 8, 1986, arrived yesterday.

Passive   The formatting of your correspondence is made easier with word processing.

Active   Word processing makes formatting your correspondence easier.

Passive   The administrative office manager is responsible for organizing and managing the flow of information. (This sentence is not strictly passive in the grammatical sense, but "is responsible" is less direct than "organizes and manages" would be.)

Active   The administrative office manager organizes and manages the flow of information.

Passive   The formal structure of an organization can be shown by an organizational chart.

Active   An organizational chart can show an organization's formal structure.

Passive   The report was filed by the clerk.

Active   The clerk filed the report.

TIP: The active voice uses fewer words than the passive voice. It is more direct and usually clearer.

EXCEPTIONS: Sometimes, you need the passive voice, depending on what you want to emphasize.

Passive   Writing letters is considered a chore today.

Active   People consider writing letters a chore today.

In a book, or letter, about writing letters, the first sentence, although passive, would be best. It puts the emphasis on the act of writing letters. The active sentence puts the emphasis on who considers writing letters a chore, which is hardly necessary, since only people write.

In the following sentences, diplomacy or tact suggests the passive voice:

Passive   Your work has been found unsatisfactory.

Active   I find your work unsatisfactory.

Passive   Smoking is prohibited.

Active   The management prohibits smoking.

Use the passive voice to communicate unpleasant news. In such situations the reader may see a direct statement as more threatening or challenging than a passive statement, and resist it accordingly. Reader resistance blocks effective communication.

At times, you may wish to remain impersonal. To do so, select the passive voice.

Be Brief

If you would be pungent, be brief; for it is with words as with sunbeams—the more they are condensed the deeper they burn.
Robert Southbey (1774–1843)

Make every word tell. Avoid unnecessary words. By being wordy, you bury your message.

Review your writing and take out those words that give the reader neither detail nor information. We use without thinking many words and phrases that clutter our message without making our point.

Use the shorter phrase. The fewer words, the more effective the communication. The examples below show some commonly used wordy phrases with brief, effective replacements:

No	*Yes*
advance planning	planning
along the lines of	like
am (are) in a position to	can
approximately about	about
are in possession of	have
assemble together	assemble
as to whether	whether
at about	about
at all times	always
at that point in time	then
the present time	now
at this point in time	now
attached herewith	attached
by means of	by
check into	check
complete monopoly	monopoly
continue on	continue
cooperate together	cooperate
customary practice	practice
depreciate in value	depreciate
due to the fact that	since (because)(as)
during the course of	during
each and every	every
economically disadvantaged	poor

enter the business world	go into business
for the purpose of	for (to)
for the reason that	because
for your information	*Do not use* (except as FYI jotted on a copy of something)
inasmuch as	since
in due course	*Do not use* (give a specific time)
in many cases	often
information of a useful character	useful information
in order to	to
in regard to	about (regarding)
in the event that	if (in case)
in the city of Boston	in Boston
in the month of May	in May
in the near future	*Do not use* (give a specific time)
make (made) the acquaintance of	meet (met)
new beginner	beginner
new record	record
notwithstanding the fact that	even though
past experience	experience
personal friend	friend
preliminary to	before
provided that	if
rarely ever	rarely
revert back	revert
service of a valuable nature	valuable service

she is a woman who is often late	she is often late
the fact that	*Do not use*
there is no doubt but that	no doubt
this is a person who	this person
with your kind permission	may

Complete Information

In your effort to be brief, however, never leave out necessary facts. Don't be like the people who sent postcards to a local television station to win prizes and left out their telephone numbers. To win, a person had to be at home and watching when the station called. Their telephone numbers were essential information.

Serial numbers, make and model, date of purchase—details, essential details—be sure to include the ones essential to your written message.

Less Is More

Not *all* information is essential. Writing everything you know about the subject—relevant and irrelevant—will confuse rather than enlighten. In your writing, do not be like those people who tell you how to build a watch when you ask them the time.

Be particularly selective when writing directions or explanations. Give the readers *everything* they need to know, but *only* what they need to know. Consider the following instructions sent with a new word processing system:

Poor   The variant is the other part of the label for a style. It is identified by a number (103 numbers are available for you to customize) or a special name (5 predefined automatic styles and 15 reserved styles).

Better   You can create 103 different styles. In addition, the system has 5 predefined styles and 15 suggested styles for your use.

In the longer paragraph, the writer said more than necessary and as a result communicated less. The information about a "variant," which turns out to be a number the system automatically assigns to styles you create, adds nothing but confusion.

The writer did not look at the subject from the reader's point of view. The reader needs or wants to know how many styles he or she can create. That the automatically assigned numbers are called "variants" is of secondary importance to the new user, and putting it in a dominant position only confuses the reader.

Be Clear

A word may be a fine-sounding word, of an unusual length, and very imposing from its learning and novelty, and yet in the connection in which it is introduced, may be quite pointless and irrelevant.

William Hazlitt (1778–1830)

Use everyday words. They will carry your message forcefully. Do not be pompous. Avoid the unfamiliar word. Also avoid jargon and foreign words unless you are sure that your reader will understand them. Always keep in mind that you are writing to "express not impress."

Below on the left is a list of pompous words that often creep into everyday writing. The plain words on the right are usually better and clearer.

No	*Yes*
adjudicate	judge
allege	say (claim)
ascertain	find out
assert	say
cease	stop
am cognizant of	know
commence	start (begin)
converse	talk

de facto	actual, in fact
demonstrate	show
endeavor	try
facilitate	help
finalize	complete (finish) (end)
fundamental	basic
inaugurate	start
initial	first
initiate	begin (start)
irregardless	regardless
institute	start
jeopardize	risk
perceive	see
peruse	read
preplanning	planning
presume	think
purport	claim (mean)
remuneration	pay (fee)
replete	full
substantiate	prove
superfluous	extra (unneeded)
supersedes	replaces
terminate	end
utilize	use

EXCEPTIONS: At times the shorter word is not the best choice:

No	*Yes*
dais	platform
edify	instruct (enlighten)
tyro	beginner
verve	energy (enthusiasm)

At times, the shorter word is not the diplomatic choice:

No	Yes
cheap	inexpensive

Be Positive and Specific

The difference between the right word and the almost right word is the difference between lightning and the lightning bug.

Mark Twain (1835–1910)

Use positive words. Avoid negative ones. Write your messages in positive forms, especially when your content is negative. This rule may be difficult to follow, but it is well worth the effort.

We do not hold reservations after 10 p.m.
We hold reservations until 10 p.m.

You cannot charge above $1000.
You can charge up to $1000.

We do not deliver on weekends.
We deliver every weekday.

You will not be sorry...
You will be pleased...

The positive form is usually shorter and more direct. When you check your writing, look for sentences with the word "not" in them. Rewrite to take it out. Often this requires nothing more than substituting a word for the "not" phrase:

did not remember	forgot
not aware	unaware
not awake	asleep
not known	unknown
not on time	late
not possible	impossible
not sure	uncertain

The message remains negative, but the terms become more forceful and direct.

Avoid or play down emotionally charged words, especially when the charge is negative. Downplay such negatively charged words as:

blame	error	mistake
cheap	failure	overreaction
complaint	fault	reject
damage	inadequate	unfortunately
defective	inferior	unreasonable

While being positive, also be specific. Avoid vague words that contain no information for your reader. Give details whenever possible:

Vague   Some parts remain in stock.
Specific   Twenty parts remain in stock.

Vague   I will send it in the near future.
Specific   I will send it on Friday.

Vague   The computer is not working properly.
Specific   The computer freezes when I hit the shift key.

COMMENT: In each example a vague word or phrase was replaced with a specific word or phrase: some equals twenty, near future equals Friday, not working properly equals freezes when I hit the shift key. If you have the fact, use it.

EXCEPTIONS: Sometimes the negative construction delivers the desired punch:

We will always remember a client.

We never forget a client.

The second sentence, cast in a negative form, is somewhat more emphatic than the first sentence.

SUMMING UP

Writing to the point does not require rare talent and extraordinary skills. Writing to communicate, not miscommunicate, is a function of a little thought and some common sense: Consider what you want to communicate, think of and involve the reader as you write, and develop these four good writing habits, which will help you shun the four bad writing habits.

This approach will take the pain and embarrassment out of writing. Try it, and discover that writing well is a gratifying and rewarding experience.

2

Write with Style

Style is more than rules of grammar and punctuation. Because it involves *choice,* style is an expression of your individuality—your personality and your attitude toward your reader and your message. In addition, a large part of style is simply the effective use of the basic structures and rules of language.

Part of your style will depend on your relationship to your reader—boss, employee, colleague, friend, relative, customer—and to your subject matter. Are you seeking information? Expressing congratulations? Requesting payment? Offering a job? Is the receiver familiar with the topic? Are you persuading, instructing, complaining? The answers to these and related questions will determine how you address your reader— whether you use formal or informal language, the "feel" of your letter—and how much and what information you include.

In this chapter, rather than list a lot of rules for memorizing, we will illustrate these rules with practical examples, using some of the most common subjects. Thus you will see the rules as an outgrowth of effective communication.

THE CARING TONE

The daughter of a colleague has recently graduated summa cum laude. You are on friendly terms with your co-worker and wish to write a note congratulating her on her daughter's success.

Poor

Dear Eileen,

I just read that Deborah was at the top of her class! You and Allen must be bursting forth with unmitigated but understandable pride. What a fine young woman she is, and what satisfaction this must mean for her parents.

We are all delighted for you. Please tell Deborah that we are every bit as proud of her as we expected to be.

Sincerely,

The letter works, but it has problems. Let's look at the ways it conveys its message effectively and at the ways it can be improved.

The opening sentence is good, introducing the subject and establishing the right tone of friendly interest between co-workers. Writing "I just read"—an informal phrase—not only establishes a relaxed tone but also imparts a sense of immediacy that, no matter what the context, will help stimulate the reader's interest.

The second sentence, unfortunately, loses most of the ground the first one gained. The phrase "bursting forth with pride" is both redundant and nonstandard. The usual phrase is "bursting with pride." Although a bit worn, at least the traditional phrase doesn't jolt the reader with an odd and awkward construction.

From the odd phrase to a shift in tone, the second sentence moves farther away from the goal of quick and easy communication. The word "unmitigated" is pompous and clashes with the rest of the letter. It does not match either the informal, conversational feel of "I just read" and "You and Allen" or the friendly closeness of "We are all delighted for you." The author has tried to liven up a familiar expression ("bursting with pride") with unexpected modifiers ("unmitigated but understandable") but has succeeded only in diluting the message. Leave the phrase alone, or do away with it, but don't try to "fix" it. The added phrase dampens the impact of the sentence, which—with "pride" in emphatic last place—would have been effective: "You and Allen must be bursting with pride." Short and sweet, and, although it may not win a prize for originality, the sentence says what it means with the fewest possible words.

The following sentences make good use of the "you" attitude, which will be discussed later in the chapter. The phrase "What a..." puts the writer in the parents' place, demonstrating empathy that is bound to please. The first clause validates the parents' pride in their daughter's accomplishments, by stating their feelings as fact. The second, employing *parallel construction* to give a sense of unity and connection, suggests that the writer shares the parents' satisfaction, without being obvious or phony. Parallel construction involves two clauses that use an identical structure. They parallel each other: "*What* a fine young woman...*what* satisfaction...."

The closing paragraph carries over the you attitude in its first sentence, making a smooth transition and helping the reader follow the train of thought. Asking to share the message with the daughter creates a feeling of warmth and sincerity that is appropriate here.

MORE ABOUT TONE

Not all your writing tasks will be as pleasant as congratulating a friend. One of the hardest letters to write is the condolence letter. It does, however, share certain qualities with the congratulatory letter: It is personal; its main purpose is to express your feelings, not information; and sincerity is of the utmost importance.

A business associate has recently died, and you must extend your sympathies to his colleagues. Here is one approach that works:

All of us at Western Electronics are grieved by the death of your president, Philip Carlos. Please accept our most sincere sympathy.

Mr. Carlos was a true leader and an example to all of us. His charitable work with the Boy Scouts of America will long be remembered.

We know that the memory of Philip Carlos will serve as an inspiration to the citizens of Green Plains.

The opening paragraph has an appropriately sympathetic, yet formal, tone. The decision to speak as a group, the choice of the rather formal word "grieved," and the use of the deceased's full name and title all contribute to that formality.

In general, avoid telling your reader how sincere you are, but this is one of the exceptions that proves the rule. Most of us understand that words simply can't do justice to a situation like this, and so we use—we even prefer—almost ritualistic assurances, such as "Please accept our most sincere sympathy."

In the next paragraph, a more personal note is introduced, but only through reflection on the subject of the letter, not as an intrusion by the writer, which would be inappropriate. The first sentence begins with a simple statement of the dead man's quality as a leader and builds to a more emphatic declaration of his effect on others. This is followed by a reference to one specific example, which *shows* that the writer is sincere and is not just mouthing platitudes.

Finally, the letter comes full circle, returning to the "we" who are writing and reiterating important points to create a sense of completion as well as sympathy and respect for the person who has died.

GETTING THINGS DONE

Much of your correspondence will not be as personal as congratulations or condolences. You will be writing to firms for information, giving instructions to workers under you, attempting to rectify others' mistakes, trying to sell a product, and so on—all the routine tasks that writing has to accomplish every day.

Giving instructions is one of the most important writing tasks you can do. Making yourself understood quickly and efficiently is particularly important when you are responsible for the result. Let's look at a couple of memos that work or don't work.

Poor

TO: All Sponsoring Editors

FROM: George Smith

SUBJECT: Quarterly Report

I have been referencing the Quarterly Report, Part 4, and I find numerous mistakes. Please work with the report very closely. In doing so I think you will see these mistakes and that our next printing of the report will be more accurate.

This report is being used by more people in the company than before. Inaccurate information is often more harmful than no information at all. This is very much a working report and Jessie can only correct what you give her.

This is a clumsy, ambiguous memo. Its effectiveness depends entirely on the readers' ability to interpret it. Let's take it apart.

> "I have been referencing the Quarterly Report, Part 4, and I find numerous mistakes."

"Referencing" is jargon and, strictly speaking, incorrect usage. Why not a simple "looking over," or "reading," if that's what the writer has been doing? A phrase such as "looking over" conveys the right meaning, and establishes an atmosphere of everyday communication that will enhance the memo's reception. Although you should avoid being artificially "folksy," a relaxed, natural tone is best in workaday communications.

"I find..." feels awkward. It is not the same tense as "I have been referencing" (or "looking over"). To parallel the first clause it should read, "*I have found...*" Also, the phrase "I find" has an aloof, lawyerly feel about it that gives the writer a snobbish air, which is counterproductive to his goal: cooperation from those under him. The next word, "numerous," adds to the pretentiousness; a word or phrase such as "a lot of," "a number of," or even just "many" would be better. But the main thing is to change "I find," and then even "numerous" might do.

> "Please work with the report very closely."

This sentence is ambiguous. Is the writer asking the reader to use the report as it is? "To work with" something, in everyday parlance, means to use it. The confusion is compounded by the phrase "working report" in the final sentence.

What the writer really means, we assume (he forces the reader to assume, which is never a good idea for a writer), is that the reader is to work *on* the report very closely; in other words, to see that mistakes are kept to a minimum. This may seem like a minor point, because we are all so used to sorting out little slips like this that we hardly notice them, but careful attention to such details reduces the friction the reader experiences and makes for a more successful message: "Please see to it that mistakes are kept to a minimum."

> "In doing so I think you will see these mistakes and that our next printing of the report will be more accurate."

This sentence should be broken into two sentences or rewritten to give the two clauses a parallel structure. But first, the writer should have a clearer idea of exactly what he's conveying. He seems to feel, and rightly so, that the previous sentence did not convey the meaning he intended, and rather than rewriting, he tried to fix it with this sentence.

He wants the reader *to prevent* mistakes in the report, but what he says is, "I think you will see these mistakes and that our next printing...will be more accurate." Besides the faulty construction, the sentence loses the main point through the cracks: The writer has never actually said, "Fix those mistakes!" A classic case of hedging.

If he had made himself clear in the previous sentence, as in the rewritten version, the writer would have a much better grip on this sentence. He can do away with the clumsy opening and unnecessary "In doing so [In doing what?] I think" and get on with the business of the sentence, which is a positive statement of what is to be accomplished by the extra effort: "I am confident that our next printing will be more accurate."

The second paragraph also forces the reader to read between the lines. The author seems to be underscoring his main points, backed up by illustrations of the importance of the project. Fine, but the lack of clarity in the first paragraph has created confusion in the second. Again, the main point—"Fix the mistakes!"—comes through only by implication.

> "This report is being used by more people in the company than before. Inaccurate information is often more harmful than no information at all."

These sentences do contain useful information, but the first one could be improved. "More people...than before" sounds funny. Perhaps the writer felt "more people...than *ever* before" sounded grandiose, in which case a phrase such as "more and more people" or "an increasing number of people" should have been substituted. As mentioned earlier, don't monkey with well-worn phrases. They got that way because they work and people like them.

Finally, active voice in general is better than passive; there is no reason this sentence can't be phrased in the active voice. In the second sentence, the use of a transitional word such as "therefore" would help give the memo flow and continuity: More and more people in the company are using this report. Inaccurate information, therefore, is often more harmful than no information at all.

> "This is very much a working report and Jessie can only correct what you give her."

The final sentence creates utter confusion with its combination of irrelevant elements. Does Jessie use this report to correct other things, as the phrasing and wording suggest? Or is Jessie a secretary preparing the report and cannot make it any better than the information the reader supplies? The statement that "Jessie can only correct what you give her" seems to invite mistakes. And did the writer really mean Jessie "can only correct" what she is given, or can correct "only what she is given?" Making people guess is not writing to the point.

The failure to be direct, combined with its generally negative tone, gives the second paragraph a whiny or petulant tone that should be avoided. Point out that the report is much in use, that inaccurate information is harmful, and then *state what needs to be done*.

Here is the memo rewritten:

TO: All Sponsoring Editors

FROM: George Smith

SUBJECT: Quarterly Report

I have been looking over the Quarterly Report, Part 4, and have found a number of mistakes. Please work closely on the report, and see to it that mistakes are kept to a minimum. I am confident that, with this extra effort on your part, our next printing will be more accurate.

More and more people in the company are using this report. Inaccurate information, therefore, is often more harmful than no information at all.

The word order in the last sentence in the first paragraph highlights the importance of "this extra effort." It breaks the clause in two, putting the "effort" between the subject and the verb, which makes it stand out. "Therefore" in the second paragraph is a connector; it refers the reader to the reasons listed in the first paragraph.

The following memo shows how a message can be conveyed directly yet fully, without a single word wasted.

TO: Project Supervisors

FROM: Arthur McBee

SUBJECT: Interim Reports

We have agreed to standardize the Interim Report for every project we accept. Please take a look at the memo about the Fowles Project Interim Report, and design a format for future reports.

Be sure to include the following information: current status of project, expected date of completion, personnel involved and their tasks, cost to date, and projected cost at completion. Any other suggestions for making these reports more effective will be appreciated.

Thank you,

The first sentence is clear and forceful. It uses the active voice and a simple construction. It includes the reader in the task by referring to an agreement already made. The memo then gives concise instructions to the reader, providing only that information the reader will need to perform the task.

The second paragraph flows smoothly from the first. The transitional device here is actually what is *not* said. "Be sure to include..." relies on the reader's memory of what has already been stated to keep things moving. Compare the effect of reiterating: "Be sure to include in the report...." It is too close; it is redundant; it blocks the flow. Here less is more.

The request for additional information in the final sentence involves the reader both through the content and the structure of the sentence. In this case the passive voice is preferred, both because "will be appreciated" is idiomatic and because it emphasizes the you attitude of the sentence.

NOTE: Every sentence except the first has "you" as its actual or understood subject, and even the first includes the reader in the general "we."

THE READER'S INTEREST

Selling (persuading) is one of the most important jobs a written message can perform, and here a direct, to-the-point efficiency and clarity are imperative. Your readers are in a hurry, have many other things to think about, and may be indifferent or even hostile to sales letters. Your job is to interest the readers immediately and convince them that what you have to say is worth reading.

In the examples that follow, consider what works and what doesn't, and see how sentences can be improved by changing *how* they are written—not *what* they say.

Dear Danielle Jones:

I recently wrote you about an important opportunity—one that could help assure your family's future security. It appears, though, that you haven't yet taken the opportunity to apply for the Acme Group Term Life Insurance Plan from Acme Life Assurance Company.

Although I initially asked that you apply by March 6, 1987, that date has been extended to March 20. So there's still time to send in your application. (Of course, if my letter and your application have crossed in the mail, there's no need to send in another application. You'll soon be hearing from Acme Life.)

What works, and what doesn't? The salutation immediately strikes a wrong note because it uses the reader's full name, which feels very impersonal. In general, if you don't know the person you are writing to, it is better to acknowledge this with the more formal "Mr." or "Ms.," which indicate respect.

The opening sentence works well. It connects reader and writer, although the reference to the earlier letter may not work if the reader has forgotten or ignored that letter. The reference does, however, establish an immediate concern for the reader's interests that will keep her reading.

The problems begin when the letter seems to accuse the reader of doing something wrong. The "you" attitude should never be negative: "You haven't taken the opportunity...." Do not assume that she *must* be interested in your message. Put yourself in the reader's position:

> "If you are like many of our customers, you may not have had time to apply for Acme Group Term Life Insurance. Fortunately, the application deadline has been extended to March 20."

This wording not only puts a positive value on your relationship with your reader but also significantly cuts the number of words—a vital concern for writing to the point.

Below is a concise, to-the-point letter selling a new book. Even if you are not interested in the book itself, you can't help getting interested in the message. Much of its appeal derives from how the words are put together.

> Communication! It's important to everyone, but it's absolutely indispensable to a businessperson like you. Good communication commands recognition, it smooths the way to promotion and higher salary, and it brings great personal satisfaction.
>
> Word power is a good place to start, of course, but good human relations, listening skills, and knowing how to target your audience are the added abilities that make words work. This is real communication skill—and it can take a lifetime to achieve it.
>
> *COMMUNICATE!* by Lynn Ashford brings you a shortcut to communicating effectively. This 150-page booklet will help you to build your basic communications skills and give you confidence to make people understand you better. Your copy of *COMMUNICATE!* is being held for you. You can pick it up at your convenience. It's only $15.95.

Notice the contrast in the structure of the first two sentences. The first is an exclamation. It is followed by a compound sentence linking two related concepts. The more important concept falls at the end—the most emphatic position in a sentence. The contrast in length gives the letter an appealing rhythm.

The third sentence provides a third contrast: another compound sentence, but this time the main idea comes first, immediately echoing the impact of the preceding sentence. Notice also how the you attitude is conveyed subtly with an appeal to goals most people share.

The transition words in the opening of the second paragraph ("a good place to start...") keep the reader moving forward. Again, the emphasis falls at the end, with three simple, but powerful, words: "make words work." Even the rhythm is forceful! The second paragraph develops the main idea of the first one—namely, what real communication entails and why it is important.

The third paragraph brings the ideas of the first two together in a way that naturally focuses on the product. Notice that, in contrast to the previous example, the name of the product isn't mentioned until the end of the letter.

The letter was effective, short, and right to the point. Most people would likely read through to the end—and get the message. Content, of course, had very little to do with the difference between these two samples: Family security is as important to most people as communication skills.

THE YOU ATTITUDE

A message offering someone money without any strings attached automatically does what an effective writer always strives to do:

PUT THE READER'S INTERESTS FIRST.

Most, if not all, of the time you write, you are not offering to give someone some money with no strings attached. Often you are asking for something or even sending some bad news, which is why you must think of the reader to write to the point. Put yourself in that person's shoes. Write your message with that person's needs and interests in mind. The better you can do this, the more effectively you will write.

This is only common sense. Consider your own reaction to people who seem to be expressing an interest and concern in what *you* want as opposed to what *they* want. You more readily accept proposals that appear to be in *your* interest. The reality, of course, is that we all look out for ourselves, but if we can show how what *we* want will help the *other* person, we are more likely to achieve our goal. Consider the following two first sentences of letters from job applicants and decide which applicant you would most likely hire:

I I am graduating from college this spring, and I am very much interested in getting the job I saw advertised. I am enclosing my résumé. I believe I would enjoy working for your excellent company. I can come for an interview next week.

YOU The job you advertised interests me very much. As you can see from my résumé, I have the training and skills you seek. I am sure I can make a meaningful contribution to your excellent company and would like very much to try. I am available for an interview at your convenience.

Play down the word "I" and other first person pronouns (we, me, my, our, us, mine, ours). Play up the word "you" and other second person pronouns (your, yours). As the samples above show, however, you shouldn't abandon words such as "I" but use them to create a "you" approach: "I would like to help you."

Another vital writing task is sharing information. This may seem rather straightforward, but how you present your information can have a tremendous impact on how it is received—with a "wow" or a yawn. If you are sharing information that someone has requested and needs, you will have that person's interest. In this case, concentrate on providing the correct information clearly and accurately.

Sometimes, providing information is part of a sales pitch or part of an attempt to persuade someone to do something. In this case, you must strive to make your message interesting to the reader. You must present your points in terms of reader needs.

Dear Personal Checking Customer:

We have good news about your Personal checking account... and new services we are adding for your convenience.

Beginning on January 1, 199_ , Personal Banks will offer improved checking accounts to better suit the diverse needs of our customers. This news could change the way you handle your Personal checking account—and help you to better manage your check-writing dollars.

Following are answers to some questions you might have about the changes taking place.

"How has my NOW or Money Market NOW checking account changed?"

We've learned from talking to consumers that they feel many bank accounts are too complicated, or may require minimum balances that are too high. So, we've simplified our NOW Account and changed its name to Flat Rate Checking. With Flat Rate Checking, there's no minimum monthly balance required (it used to be $1000). So now you can access more of your cash when you need it. And, you will earn a competitive interest rate of 4.88 percent. That yields a nice round 5 percent each year on your balance.

With Flat Rate Checking you'll find balancing your checkbook is easier than ever, because there's only one $3 fee per month. (In the past, NOW Account customers paid $6 or $8 fees if their account balances dropped below $1000.) This new low fee *never changes* from month to month—regardless of your balance or the number of checks you write.

We've also improved our Money Market NOW Account and renamed it Ultra NOW Checking. With Ultra NOW Checking, the opening deposit and minimum monthly balance is now only $1000 (it used to be $2500).

Ultra NOW Checking will continue to offer *competitive market interest rates*. There is no regular monthly fee—although there is a $10 charge if the average balance for any monthly statement period falls below $1000.

"With these changes taking place, will I have to get new checks or change my account number?"

No, we've taken care of everything. You can continue using your current checks, and your account number will *not* change.

"What else is new at Personal?"

We have recently enhanced our services to make banking easier for you. We've expanded our telephone banking hours to serve you *24 hours a day, 7 days a week*. So now, you can talk to our friendly and knowledgeable consultants around the clock to get general information such as rates and branch locations or to discuss Personal accounts and services. All this, so you can bank when it's convenient for *you!*

The you attitude here is obvious, and effective. The letter has been constructed to emphasize how the changes will benefit the reader. The choice of words is neither too pompous nor too chatty; the letter has a natural, easy tone that does not call attention to itself.

Information is presented concisely. Ideas and facts are arranged according to their importance and their relationship to each other.

The question-and-answer format intensifies the you approach. Notice how the first answer moves logically from the problem—bank accounts are too complicated—to the solution.

The general statement of the solution is followed by specific information explaining how the new system differs from the old. No unnecessary information clutters the paragraph. A related concept is introduced in a new paragraph.

This is a long letter, close to being too long, but it works. Breaking the subject into small, related chunks makes reading easier. The receiver can absorb small bits of information at a time, and with so many distractions competing for your readers' attention, this is a good way to write to the point.

The letter uses the technique of different sentence structures, although here it is less pronounced than in the previous example. In general, the subject-verb-object "core" of each sentence occurs at the beginning, which is appropriate when simply conveying information. A dull, thudding quality is avoided, however, through the occasional use of prepositional phrases ("With Flat Rate Checking," "In the past,"), subordinate clauses ("We've learned from talking to customers that..."), and so on.

Notice the use of parallel constructions to highlight related pieces of information. The phrase "With Flat Rate Checking" is echoed by the next paragraph's "With Ultra NOW Checking," which emphasizes the similarity of the *type* of information being presented.

Repetition of key words, phrases, and ideas helps connect different but related portions of the letter. This is often better than trying to avoid using the same word twice, because it recalls what has already been said and helps fix it in the reader's mind. Some words and phrases appearing more than once are: "news," "changes," "it used to be..." ("In the past" echoes the thought without being *too* repetitive), and "so" or "so now." These connect the sentences to each other and to the overall idea of the letter.

Finally, transitional words and phrases perform the same connecting function: "*This news* could change," "We've *also* improved," "With *these* changes taking place." Effective transitions are especially important in this letter, where making a smooth transition is the *subject* of the letter as well.

MORE ABOUT YOU AND I

Below are some common "I"-focused phrases (left column) with examples of how they can be easily changed to "you"-focused phrases (right column):

I want to thank you	Thank you
I am applying for	[Will you] Please consider me for
I need your help	Your help will
Our service will	Your needs will
My idea is	What do you think
We need your reply by	Please send your reply by

Along with using the pronoun "you," make your writing more personal by using the name of your receiver: Bill, what do you think...? Use the name as you would in speaking: If you are on a first name basis, use it; if not, use the second name and proper title. (See material on salutations in Chapter 5.)

Do not use the person's full name in the salutation:

Avoid   Dear Susan M. Holmes
Use   Dear Ms. Holmes (or whatever the correct title is)

Never use the person's full name and title in the text:

Avoid   We are happy to tell you, Ms. Susan M. Holmes, that you...

These attempts to personalize a message reek of phoniness and a very impersonal computer.

Exceptions

You must use "I" and other first person pronouns from time to time. Sometimes use the "I" for warmth and impact:

I congratulate you

I offer you

I am proud of you.

Use "I"—but use it sparingly.

Caution

Use "you" naturally as you do when talking. Too many "you's" will send a message of insincerity.

Avoid   Your free book will show you how you can get off on the right foot. Once you receive your free book, look it over. It's your complete guide to your learning without frustration. Once you see how your free book simplifies your learning, you'll be convinced that this is the series for you.

Better   The free book will show you how to get off on the right foot. It's a complete guide to learning without frustration. Once you see how the free book simplifies learning, you'll be convinced that this is the series for you.

Use the person's name once or twice. Do not pepper the page with the person's name. When used naturally, a name lends warmth and a personal touch. When used unnaturally, names give the message a ring of insincerity.

THE VOICE OF AUTHORITY

A complaint letter can do one of two things: it can let off steam, or it can try to get a problem fixed. It is a rare letter that can do both.

When writing a complaint, be sure you know which it is you want to do. Generally, you will be trying to get your reader to do something for you to get a problem fixed. In this case, you will want to write in a way that will accomplish your goal, not just tell the reader how you feel.

Compare the two samples below. Both have the same purpose, but one is much more effective than the other.

Poor

Dear Mrs. Carson:

I was very disappointed and angry to have the raisins in my cake mix sink to the bottom. It was especially infuriating because my bridge club had no dessert because of your rotten product.

Don't you think you owe me an apology and money for a defective product?

Better

Dear Mrs. Carson:

I am sure you will want to know that the raisins in your Streusel Coffee Cake Mix sink to and settle at the bottom of the cake when baked.

Will you please tell me why this might have happened? I realize there are several possible explanations. My supplier may have kept the mix on the shelf too long, or I may not have followed the directions correctly. At any rate, I want to know so that I can restore my faith in Streusel Mixes, which have long been a family favorite.

The main difference between the two samples is that the first is relentlessly negative in tone, whereas the second seeks to establish a connection with the reader. In a situation such as this, it is in Mrs. Carson's interest to be attentive to your needs, even to anticipate them somewhat. You needn't spell it out for her. She knows that she owes you an apology. ("The customer is always right.") Knowing this, you can afford to be friendly, which is more likely to produce a cooperative response.

A second major difference between the two is in the sentences themselves. The second uses clear, consistent language that helps get the message across. The first uses language that clashes with itself.

Let's suppose you really do just want to vent your frustration, and you don't really care about getting a reaction—your faith in Streusel is already shot. How can the first letter's construction be improved?

The first sentence begins in a "narrative" mode ("I *was* very disappointed..."), then shifts abruptly to a more abstract mode ("*to have* the raisins...*sink*"). Make the whole sentence narrative:

> "I was very disappointed *when* the raisins in your cake mix *sank* to the bottom."

Now the sentence has some force. It also parallels the construction of the second sentence, giving the whole paragraph the immediacy of a story.

Two "becauses" in the second sentence are confusing, distracting, and unnecessary. "Your rotten product" is too shrill even for letting off steam; the phrase sounds childish and actually saps the strength of your complaint. Compare: "It was especially infuriating because my bridge club had no dessert as a result."

"Don't you think" invites the reader to disagree. Substitute "I'm sure you will agree." This phrase includes the reader without leaving room for dissent. The writer speaks with the voice of authority. Finally, "money for a defective product" is a refund. Say so.

Our sample now reads:

I was very disappointed when the raisins in your cake mix sank to the bottom. It was especially infuriating because my bridge club had no dessert as a result.

I'm sure you will agree that you owe me an apology and a refund.

You may still prefer the nice approach, but at least the angry letter feels authoritative now, not childish and ineffectual. It might even get some results!

BE POSITIVE AND DIRECT

Often you will need to convey bad news in a letter. If you can't pay or are refusing credit, your task will not be easy. Express negative messages in positive terms, but don't beat around the bush. Confusion doesn't soften the blow, it makes it worse.

Let's say a person has asked for credit from your firm, and you have found that the individual does not qualify. How can you say this clearly in a positive tone without giving false hope or seeming patronizing?

Dear Mr. Keenan:

Thank you for your kind remarks about our new catalog and for being a regular cash-purchase customer for more than 10 years.

You have remained a cash customer for so many years, we are sure, because of our low prices and quality merchandise. Savings to customers, however, are possible only when losses are low.

To protect ourselves from losses, thereby ensuring low prices and greater savings to our customers, we grant credit only to those who earn a minimum of $300 weekly. When your weekly income reaches the $300 minimum, we will enthusiastically grant you credit.

Until then, take advantage of the great savings for both cash and credit customers at our Krazy Days Sale beginning Saturday, June 10.

Notice how the letter begins with an appreciation of the reader's enthusiasm and long patronage. It then moves logically to the reason for the refusal, making effective use of transitional devices ("so many years," repetition of "losses" and "savings").

Only after the reasons have been explained clearly and fully does the writer explain that credit cannot be granted. Thus, the refusal becomes a necessary conclusion to factors the company must consider. By helping the reader to understand your position in this way, you soften the blow without hedging. The explanation is directly connected to the refusal and seems less a personal rejection.

The refusal itself is phrased positively: "*When* your weekly income reaches the $300 minimum, we *will* enthusiastically grant you credit.'' The reader is not tempted to take the refusal personally.

Not being able to pay a bill is a classic case of needing to express a negative message in positive language. Delivering bad news is always a delicate matter. Make sure the way you deliver it doesn't make the receiver wish for the days when the bearer of bad tidings was executed.

In this example, you have acquired a hospital bill of $300 that you cannot pay off all at once. You would like to spread the payment out over a period of 6 months.

Dear Ms. Smart:

Regarding my hospital bill from 4/28/89, I would like to suggest the following.

If you will accept $50 a month, we can clear up the balance in 6 months.

I trust this will be satisfactory for you, and look forward to your response.

The letter doesn't hedge. It is short, to the point, and expresses its essentially negative idea (''I can't pay'') in positive terms: ''I *will* pay *in six months*.'' It also stresses its concern for the reader's interests: ''If you will accept,'' ''satisfactory to you.''

I'M THE ONE FOR YOU

Writing that can have a profound impact on your future is the ''fishing'' letter seeking employment. The fishing letter requires a deft combination of several elements. The letter must deliver information effectively; it must reflect others' needs while concentrating on yourself; it must convey something of your personality in a way that will appeal to a potential employer. How you balance these elements will determine your success as a job hunter. What do you think of the following example?

Dear Mr. Smith:

Mrs. Rosemary Blackstone, my office coordinator, has informed me of a secretarial vacancy in your firm. Please consider me an applicant.

I graduate June 4 from St. Louis Park Senior High School, where I maintained a B average and an excellent attendance record. During my senior year, I was selected from among 100 applicants to participate in the Office Education Cooperative Training Program. This allowed me to gain on-the-job experience every afternoon after school. As you might expect, this dual role of student and worker made it necessary for me to mature quickly.

As you will notice on my enclosed résumé, I have participated in several extracurricular activities. A most challenging one was raising $5000 for our office vocational youth activities. Involvement, teamwork, and responsibility have more meaning for me because of these activities.

On-the-job training for the Liberty Insurance Company included filing, record keeping, and mail room work. As relief receptionist, I received calls and greeted visitors, referring them as necessary.

Mr. John Jacobs, office manager for Liberty Insurance Company, and others listed on my résumé have given me permission to use them for references. You may call or write them for further information concerning my character and work skills.

Will you please grant me an interview? You may reach me by letter or call me at (612) 937-2800 after 4:30 p.m. if you wish.

Sincerely,

Pamela J. Eckers

The letter begins with a straightforward statement of purpose. The second paragraph gets right down to business, giving the applicant's educational and employment history in a context relevant to the subject. Pamela does not mention, for example, how she did in chemistry class or whether she was a football fan. Performance and activities are mentioned only insofar as they relate to the job.

The paragraphs are arranged logically, with the most important and most general information first and details second. The reader knows that Pamela is organized, not one to waste time. Again, the *way* you say something can get a message across better than *what* you say. Suppose Pamela had *told* the reader that she is organized and efficient. The reader may or may not believe her, but most readers would be at least a little skeptical: "Easier said than done." But this letter *shows* that Pamela is organized, without her having to mention these qualities.

Pamela has made herself an attractive applicant with this letter in other ways. She knows that the reader wants a mature employee. That won't show up on her resume, though. Should she just wait for the interview to demonstrate her maturity? No. She does not simply tell the reader that she is mature, she shows *why* she has this important trait. She brings the information to the reader in a believable form. Throughout the letter, she has tailored the information and its presentation to the needs of her future employer to demonstrate that she "fits the bill" perfectly.

To sum up, remember these important points:

- Condense as much as possible, highlighting the important points. Use sentences that are businesslike, achieving their goals with a minimum of waste. Enclose a résumé with your letter to present your history.

- Put what you say about yourself in the reader's perspective. Try to anticipate the needs and goals of the company to which you are writing.

- Let your style reflect those aspects of yourself that are desirable traits in an employee. This does *not* mean being cute, a comedian, or a "pal." Traits your friends appreciate in you may not interest an employer looking for efficiency, intelligence, compatibility. Make your message show that you have these qualities. Don't use language that sounds childish or inappropriate.

STANDING OUT FROM THE CROWD

Thank-you letters are among the most often written. Etiquette, not to mention common decency, requires such letters for gifts received on many different occasions, for favors done, to hosts for providing a pleasant weekend.

A particularly important thank-you letter is the one you should write to follow up a job interview. This letter, which should be quite brief, demonstrates an active interest in the position and helps you stand out from the crowd. (For more on the follow-up letter, see Chapter 11.)

Dear Ms. Matheson:

Thank you for taking the time last week to talk with me about the teller position at your Shady Lane branch.

Our interview confirmed my impression that I would very much enjoy working at Personal Bank. It was delightful to meet such a friendly and cooperative group of people. I'd like to be a part of that!

I look forward to hearing from you when you have made a final decision. Once again, thank you for your time and interest.

As you can see, the letter is more concerned with making contact than with providing any new information. It is not trying too hard to persuade the reader to do anything. The reader knows what you want and has all the information on your résumé. Your task is to reinforce a good impression and remind the reader of your desire to get the job.

The first paragraph is one sentence long, a simple sentence that says "thank you" and reminds Ms. Matheson of who is writing to her. The next paragraph demonstrates a sense of identification with the job and the people at the job that is likely to impress her favorably.

Finally, the letter uses a sincere closing, neither coy nor pushy, looking forward to good news. All the sentences are declaratives, most simple, one or two complex. They convey a feeling of interest in the reader, which is the most important thing any written message has to do.

HUMOR, SARCASM, ANGER: BEWARE

Humor and sarcasm are difficult to convey in writing. Readers often misunderstand humor. Sarcasm frequently backfires. In general, avoid them—particularly sarcasm.

Your writing should not be somber, though. Do try for a light touch—but keep it light. If you are writing either a personal or business letter to an individual you know and understand, you might use humor successfully. You might even try sarcasm in a personal letter. To succeed at all, sarcasm requires that writer and reader know each other rather well. Avoid the urge to be sarcastic in a business or nonpersonal letter.

When angry, go ahead and write. Get it out of your system. Do not, however, send what you wrote. Put it away for a while. Then get it out and rewrite it.

If you write when angry, you are less likely to achieve your goal (assuming it is something more than merely expressing anger). Angry letters generally stimulate nothing more than angry reactions.

There are times, though, when you are angry and all you want is to let someone know that. You are not looking to stimulate any action and you are prepared to accept the reactive anger. In such situations, let yourself go. You might even try humor and sarcasm, which can be effective tools of anger.

A classic angry letter reportedly written by a congressman to an annoying constituent consisted of this one sentence:

Dear Sir,

I thought you would like to know that some idiot has been writing me letters and signing your name to them.

Sincerely,

Another small gem that insulted with just the right touch:

Dear Sir:

I am sitting in the smallest room in the house. I have your review in front of me. Soon it will be behind me.

Sincerely,

(Source: Max Reger, 1873–1916, quoted in "The Third 637 Best Things" from *New York Magazine,* July 8, 1974.)

SUMMING UP

Yes, you must be aware of and use the basic structures and rules of language to write effectively, but what you want to say, your relationship with your reader, what you want to show of your personality and individuality—these are the ingredients of an effective writing style.

3

Putting Words in Their Place

To write effectively, you must think of what you want to say, the words to use, and the order in which to put the words. (This is also true of speaking.) You must organize your thoughts, and your writing should reflect that organization.

Fortunately, all languages have logical patterns that help us to organize our words and help the recipient of our message to understand it.

You can express an idea in one of four grammatical units: a word, a phrase, a clause, or a sentence. You begin with a word and then combine it with another word to create a *phrase*. You put phrases together to form a *clause*. With one or more clauses you create a *sentence*. You combine sentences to form a *paragraph,* and paragraphs to form your letter, report, or memo.

TAKE GRAMMAR EASILY

You do not need to know a lot of rules of grammar to write well. All you need know is what makes sense based upon common usage. Some rules are necessary, because if we did not agree on meaning, we could not communicate; rules help give meaning to words. Because of its history of borrowing from different languages, however, English is a very irregular language. Its rules have many exceptions and provide only a rough guideline. Do not paralyze yourself struggling to follow rules of grammar.

Word order is important, and so are sentences, paragraphs, and punctuation. In this chapter, you will find what you should know about word order, sentences, and paragraphs. In Chapter 4, you will find everything you need to know about that pesky punctuation.

SENTENCES

The effectiveness of your written message depends on the structure of your sentences. The right words are necessary, but the order in which you place them in sentences determines how well they will do their job.

Construct your sentences with care. Do not, however, become self-conscious about them. You speak in sentences naturally. Write in them naturally. Do not begin any writing thinking "Now I am writing, I must be aware of all the rules of grammar."

Just write. Write your message as you would say it. *Then* go back and rewrite. You will form your best sentences thinking of *what* you want to say, rather than *how* you want to say it. When you have the *what* of your message down, concentrate on *how you will say it.*

Ultimately, all good, clear writing comes from rewriting. Rarely is a first effort good enough to send. You will read this advice often. Take it to heart. Remember the words of Samuel Johnson: "What is written without effort is in general read without pleasure." (And, you could add, without understanding.)

Importance of Word Order

In English, the position of words is a major factor in establishing their meaning. These simple sentences illustrate how a word's position determines the meaning of the sentence:

She saw through the operation.

She saw the operation through.

He looked over the paper.

He looked the paper over.

He overlooked the paper.

The general order in which words are placed is decided by rules of grammar and by a writer's preference or style. For example, as noted earlier, the usual order is subject-verb-object (or complement):

The prices went down.

Sometimes we invert the order for special emphasis, complement-verb-subject:

Down went the prices.

The position of *modifiers* (words that explain or define other words) is particularly important. Keep modifiers close to the words they modify. Failure to follow this placement is a common mistake that often results in miscommunication. See what the faulty placement of modifiers does to meaning in these examples:

Faulty   Being cracked, I am returning this plate to you.

Correct   I am returning this cracked plate to you.

Faulty   After being promoted, my boss explained my new duties to me.

Correct   After I was promoted, my boss explained my new duties to me. Or: My boss explained my new duties to me after I was promoted.

Faulty   After 10 days the clerk said I could return the merchandise if not satisfied.

Correct   I could return the merchandise after 10 days if not satisfied, the clerk said. Or: The clerk said I could return the merchandise after 10 days, if not satisfied. (Use of punctuation to make this sentence clear is described in Chapter 4.)

Writing Effective Sentences

Here are some simple tips for keeping your sentences effective.

Vary the Length of Your Sentences

Sentences of varied lengths make for pleasant, easier reading. Avoid lengthy sentences. Twenty words is considered a good average sentence, but there is no fixed rule. Keep sentences short, but not choppy. Consider these opening sentences, from an essay by Kim Stafford, that range in length from 6 words to 25. The varying lengths help make the passage interesting.

> *My workbench is a writhing bundle of stories. It sports salty driftwood that crossed the pond, and salvage boards from the day they leveled my sister's house. By a trestle up the Gorge, I plucked for a shelf a clear fir stair-tread that flipped off a train. There is the sweet pine plank pulled clean from the Camp Sherman dump, and the stub-beam worktop one penitent carpenter dropped off before dawn. He owed us money, but paid us in boards. By wood's magic, that bench fits.*
>
> ("Pine, Fir, Cedar, Yew," in *Having Everything Right*, Confluence Press, Lewiston, Idaho, 1986, p. 93.)

Don't Shift Gears in Mid-Sentence

Be consistent: Use the same construction to express related ideas (parallel construction). Parallel construction helps the reader to see the relationship of ideas. Writers often fail to use parallel construction and thus shift a sentence's point of view or its verb form, which confuses the reader. For example:

Shifted   Do not ignore traffic signals and stay within the speed limit.

Parallel   Do not ignore traffic signals and do not speed.

The shift from a negative to a positive in the first sentence's point of view makes the sentence's meaning fuzzy. Keeping the construction parallel makes the meaning unmistakable.

Shifted   Detailed instructions are enclosed, and it will be done in a few hours.

Parallel   Detailed instructions are enclosed, and they will help you do the job in a few hours.

In the first sentence, the subject shifts from "instructions" to "job," giving the impression that just reading the instructions will take a few hours.

Shifted First turn on the computer, and then you should decide which program to use.

Parallel First turn on the computer, and then decide which program to use.

If giving instructions, give them. Do not encourage doubts by shifting from direct ("decide") to conditional ("you should decide") statements.

Shifted The power failure lasted several hours, and it was the cause of much ruined food.

Parallel The power failure lasted several hours and caused much food to be ruined. Or: The power failure lasted several hours and ruined much food.

The voice shifted from active to passive in the shifted example.
Parallel construction shows the relationship of ideas vividly and helps the reader understand the message.

Be Emphatic Wisely

Before resorting to mechanical devices for emphasis, use the natural flow of your sentences to achieve impact. The order in which you arrange your words is important:

THE MOST EMPHATIC POSITION IS AT THE END OF THE
SENTENCE. THE SECOND MOST EMPHATIC POSITION IS THE
BEGINNING OF THE SENTENCE.

Do not dull the impact of the beginning of your sentences by putting in unnecessary words. Start quickly.

Dull There is no product superior to Zingo in the marketplace.

Emphatic No product in the marketplace is superior to Zingo.
Zingo is superior to all products in the marketplace.

Dull I feel it fitting to submit another high-quality manuscript to your publishing group.

Emphatic I submit another high-quality manuscript to your publishing group.

Dull It is incumbent upon you to prepare for your participation in these meetings that will be held next month.

Emphatic You must prepare for next month's meetings. Or: [Please] Prepare for next month's meetings.

TIP: Avoid starting sentences with weak phrases such as "There is," "There are," "It is," "Inasmuch as," and "This is to."

Sentences should build to a natural climax. Don't put the ending in the middle.

Dull The merchandise was defective that you sent me.

Emphatic The merchandise that you sent me was defective.

Dull We are promoting you to manager, because of your excellent work.

Emphatic Because of your excellent work, we are promoting you to manager.

Dull Please do not wait until the last day or two to prepare for this meeting.

Emphatic Please do not wait until a day or two before this meeting to prepare. Or: Please do not wait until just before this meeting to prepare.

Dull You will find our services timely, effective, and essential, and our prices reasonable if you compare them to others.

Emphatic You will find our services timely, effective, essential, and reasonably priced.

Be Careful With Mechanical Devices for Emphasis

Many mechanical devices can emphasize what you write. Be stingy about using them. Overuse blunts their effectiveness.

Mechanical devices include <u>underlining words</u>, USING ALL CAPITALS, and emphatic punctuation, mainly the exclamation point (!), but also dashes (—).

Certain words, known as *intensives,* can also be used for emphasis: much, very, such, too, highly, certainly, extremely, tremendously. Be careful in your use of these. Do not sprinkle them throughout your writing. The same holds true for superlatives, as you read in Chapter 1.

PARAGRAPHS

Organize sentences into paragraphs. Paragraphs in ordinary writing average five sentences. They can be only one sentence, or they can be longer. If too long, they do not accomplish their basic mission, which is to organize your message so the reader can understand it easily.

Using paragraphs also helps you write by forcing you to put your information down logically a bit at a time. Our ideas do not come to us in an orderly, organized way. They rush or creep into our heads in no particular order. You must put your ideas in order—first into sentences and then into paragraphs—to indicate degrees of relationship and a logical sequence.

Paragraphs allow you to convey your message in separated, manageable bits of closely related information. The first line of a paragraph is usually indented, and extra space is usually before and after each paragraph. These breaks between paragraphs make reading a page easier.

To develop paragraphs, think of what you want to say—your major topic. Then break it down into smaller component topics, each of which would be one or more paragraphs.

Paragraph Structure

Paragraphs, like sentences, have a typical structure. The first and last sentences are the more emphatic parts. The paragraph structure contains three basic parts: (1) topic sentence, (2) detail (middle sentences), and (3) summary sentence.

The Topic Sentence

This is usually the first or introductory sentence of a paragraph. The topic sentence tells the reader in a general way what the paragraph is about.

If the topic sentence is the introductory sentence, it should make a smooth transition from the previous paragraph by showing the connection. (See discussion of transitions later in this chapter.) The topic sentence can appear in the middle of the paragraph and even at the end.

The Middle Sentences

These are the substance of the paragraph. The sentences in the middle of the paragraph carry the specific detail to support the topic.

The Summary Sentence

This is usually the final sentence. The summary brings the detail together and concisely relates it to the topic or the point the writer wants the reader to remember. It should begin the transition to the next paragraph.

Sometimes, for emphasis, a writer will begin with the details, building up to the summation and concise statement of the topic. Sometimes the summary and topic sentence are the same. Consider the following memo:

Poor

TO: All Employees   FROM: Personnel

SUBJECT: Summer Hours   DATE: May 1, 19_

There is a need to develop a plan for summer hours that is not disruptive to the company's operations. Last year's practice of closing early on Fridays during July and August did not work satisfactorily and will not be continued this year. The directors feel that there should be some relief during the hot summer months. We propose each employee be permitted to take every second Friday off. Schedules must be set so that half the office force is at work every Friday. To make up the "lost" time, each employee is required to extend their working hours by one hour each day. It is worth remembering that summer hours are a privilege and a benefit provided by the company. Even though the working hours "given up" are in fact regained by extending the regular working day, there is still a disruptive effect. This is only a proposal and will not become policy until each of you has had an opportunity to consider it. All concerns or comments will be considered, but a decision must be made no later than Tuesday, June 24.

Several things are wrong with this memo. As a first step toward fixing it, let's break it into paragraphs. Simply doing this makes it easier to read.

Better

TO: All Employees   FROM: Personnel

SUBJECT: Summer Hours   DATE: June 1, 19_

There is a need to develop a plan for summer hours that is not disruptive to the company's operations. Last year's practice of closing early on Fridays during July and August did not work satisfactorily and will not be continued this year.

The directors feel that there should be some relief during the hot summer months. We propose each employee be permitted to take every second Friday off.

Schedules must be set so that half the office force is at work every Friday. To make up the "lost" time, each employee is required to extend his or her working hours by one hour each day.

It is worth remembering that summer hours are a privilege and a benefit provided by the company. Even though the working hours "given up" are in fact regained by extending the regular working day, there is still a disruptive effect.

This is only a proposal, and it will not become policy until each of you has had an opportunity to consider it. All concerns or comments will be considered, but a decision must be made no later than Tuesday, June 24.

TRANSITIONS

A common writing flaw is failing to connect paragraphs. Although paragraphs present different aspects of the overall topic, they are all related. Make this relationship clear. Build on what has gone before. Stress the connection with the previous paragraph or with the overall topic.

You can show the transition or relationship between paragraphs in two ways:

1. By repeating key words, or ideas in different words

2. By using transitional words and phrases

Many transitional words and phrases help the reader move easily from one aspect of the topic to the next. Here are some samples:

accordingly	another reason
as a result	besides
even though	hence
however	in the second place
on the contrary	on the other hand
otherwise	meanwhile
nevertheless	therefore

In the sample memo on summer hours, paragraphs and sentences often begin as if nothing had come before them. Adding transitions to the summer hour memo helps move the thoughts along and connects them.

Better

TO: All Employees   FROM: Personnel

SUBJECT: Summer Hours   DATE: June 1, 19_

There is a need to develop a plan for summer hours that is not disruptive to the company's operations. Last year's practice of closing early on Fridays during July and August did not work satisfactorily and will not be continued this year.

The directors feel, *however,* that there should be some relief during the hot summer months. We propose, *therefore, that* each employee be permitted to take every second Friday off.

To minimize disruption, schedules must be set so that half the office force is at work every Friday. To make up *for the Friday off* ~~"lost" time~~, each employee is required to extend his or her working hours by one hour each day.

It is worth remembering that *summer hours* are a privilege and a benefit provided by the company. Even though the working hours "given up" are in fact regained by extending the regular working day, there is still a disruptive effect.

This is only a proposal *for summer hours,* and it will not become policy until each of you has had an opportunity to consider it. All concerns or comments will be considered, but a decision must be made no later than Tuesday, June 24.

Note how the italicized words (most of which were added) connect the various paragraphs and increase readability. Continuity was achieved either by using transitional words or by repeating subject words.

The memo is still not very good because it violates other good writing practices. When reading it, did you feel it was negative? Also, it expresses more interest in "I" than "you." Let's rewrite to make it more positive and to instill a "you" attitude.

Better

TO: All Employees   FROM: Personnel

SUBJECT: Summer Hours   DATE: June 1, 19_

~~There is a need~~ *The company wants your reaction to a plan* for summer hours *that is fair to all and* not disruptive of the company's operations. Last year's practice of closing early on Fridays during July and August did not work satisfactorily and will not be continued this year.

The directors feel, however, that *employees should have* some relief during the hot summer months. We propose, therefore, that each employee be permitted to take every second Friday off.

To minimize disruption, schedules must be set so that half the office force is at work every Friday. To make up for the Friday off, each employee *will be asked* ~~is required~~ to extend his or her working hours by one hour each day.

Please ~~It is worth~~ remember~~ing~~ that summer hours are a privilege and a benefit ~~provided by the company.~~ Even though the working hours "given up" are ~~in fact~~ regained by extending the regular working day, there is still a disruptive effect.

Your reaction and comments will be appreciated. This is only a proposal for summer hours and it will not become policy until each of you has had an opportunity to ~~consider~~ *review* it *and respond.* All concerns or comments will be considered. *Please respond* ~~but a decision must be made~~ no later than Tuesday, June 24.

The italicized words and the deletions help soften the negative feeling of the original memo and give it more of a you attitude.

First and Last Paragraphs

Your first and last paragraphs are the most important ones you write. Take pains with them. You will almost always need to rewrite them.

First Paragraphs

Your first paragraph should put forth your theme or reason for writing. Don't lead up to your subject—start with it immediately. Trying to introduce or lead up to a topic is a common mistake in writing. Often when you read over what you have written, you will find that your topic jumps into focus in your second or third paragraph. Make this your first paragraph in your revision.

The first paragraph should capture the reader's interest and therefore should reflect a you attitude. State your topic in terms of what most interests the reader.

Let's say you are planning to take a class at the local community college and you want information on schedules, tuition, and so on. Here is an example that wastes the reader's time with an unnecessary introduction:

To whom it may concern:

I am a 33-year-old college graduate currently working at the local branch of the First International Bank. Because I work 9 to 5, my schedule prevents me from taking classes at the normal time. I would therefore like to know if you have classes available for adults in the evening.

I would like to sign up for an intermediate class in word processing for the spring semester. Please send me information about when such classes will be offered, the cost, and any necessary application forms.

The writer probably thought that she needed to explain her situation to the admissions office before they would understand her request. If she had put herself in her reader's position, she would have realized that they get many requests like this and understand the situation quite well. She should have reversed the order of the paragraphs and cut the explanations to the essentials: the hours she is available. Here is the improved version:

I would like to sign up for an intermediate class in word processing for the spring semester. Please send me information about when such classes will be offered, the cost, and the necessary application forms.

My schedule prevents me from taking classes during the day. I would therefore like to know what you have available in the evening.

One reason letters are often cluttered with unnecessary introductions is that sometimes you need to write a little before you really hit your stride. These initial remarks are more for your own benefit, like taking several deep breaths before starting a race. Once you've hit your stride and are saying what you *really* want to say, go back and take out the false starts.

Middle Paragraphs

Middle paragraphs carry the bulk of your facts. They should support and reinforce the first paragraph while preparing your reader for the last paragraph. After capturing the reader's interest, build on it by presenting your facts in a logical sequence.

Last Paragraphs

In the last paragraph, sum up. Drive your point home. If you want action, now is the time to ask for it.

Don't waste your final paragraph by making it a grab bag of minor details you did not put into the body of your writing. And don't waste it apologizing for what you have or have not written.

Consider a complaint letter in which you are seeking a refund or replacement. You have already spelled out the problem in your opening paragraph and supported your case in the middle paragraph(s) with the necessary details. Now you want to leave your reader with a forceful impression that she or he had better act to retain your goodwill. Here is an example of an effective closing paragraph:

> I am sure that you understand my irritation, and will act quickly to correct the mistake. You have a reputation for service that you no doubt wish to maintain. I look forward to hearing from you by the thirtieth.

Make the summation concise and pointed. It should not be a word-for-word repeat of what has gone before. Round out your ideas and bring them to the specific point you want the reader to take away.

SUMMING UP

Okay, you *do* need to know something about grammar to write to the point, but begin with what *you* want to say and how *you* want to say it. Then call on grammar and an awareness of sentence structure and word order to say it effectively. And the best, easiest, least painful way to do this is by rewriting. Write what you want to say; read it over as if you are the person you want to reach, and then rewrite it.

4

Punctuation, Spelling, Legibility

In this chapter you will learn why punctuation is practical, why spelling is important, and why legibility is necessary. Material marked with FYI (for your information) is good to know, but not essential.

THAT PESKY PUNCTUATION

People at one time did not worry much about punctuation. They thought so little of it thattheydidnotevenbothertoputspacesbetween theirwords. Then they began to realize that spaces between words made reading easier, which helped get their messages across. Eventually they found that by using little dots, dots with tails, and other marks they could make the meaning of their written message even clearer.

Punctuate Naturally

There is nothing mysterious about punctuation. Essentially, it does in writing what we do naturally when we talk—pauses occasionally to give the receiver of our message time to understand it. Punctuation means putting in pauses. Pauses also help show the relationship between adjacent words.

Some teachers with well-meaning but misguided zeal have infected many people with what could be called "comma anxiety." These teachers teach punctuation as if it were based on some hard-to-grasp, ironclad rules.

Without rules, we would not understand each other, but many rules are flexible, and the important rule is easy to understand:

> IF THE PUNCTUATION HELPS YOUR MEANING, USE IT.
> IF IT DOESN'T, DON'T.

TIP: To determine if the punctuation helps, read your sentence out loud. If your voice drops or you pause naturally at the punctuation, it is probably doing the job.

A punctuation mark indicates a pause. Different marks stand for different degrees of pauses: a full pause (or stop), a half pause, and a slight pause.

Full-Pause Punctuation

The *period* (.) is the most-used punctuation for a full stop. It marks the end of a sentence. You have delivered a full thought, so you make a full stop before moving on to the next related thought.

The *question mark* (?) and the *exclamation point* (!) also indicate a full stop and the end of a sentence. The type of sentence

---

PUNCTUATION MARKS

There are not many punctuation marks. Those you will use with any degree of regularity are:

'	Apostrophe	—	Dash
*	Asterisk	( )	Parentheses
:	Colon	.	Period
,	Comma	?	Question mark
...	Ellipsis	" "	Quotation marks
!	Exclamation point	;	Semicolon
-	Hyphen		

determines when these marks are used. The question mark is used with an interrogative sentence: "What are the quarterly sales figures?" "How much is it?" An exclamation point ends an exclamatory sentence, such as "We won!" "It's a girl!" (An exclamatory sentence makes an emphatic statement.)

TIP: Use the exclamation point sparingly. It will not give a flabby sentence punch, and it might make readers feel you are trying to con them. Exclamation points work best with short sentences: "Help!" "Good Luck!"

Half-Pause Punctuation

The *semicolon* (;) indicates a pause somewhere between a period and a comma (see "Slight-Pause Punctuation" below). It usually separates two clauses that are capable of standing alone as independent sentences but are closely enough related to be included in one sentence. In this case, it should not be used with a coordinating conjunction, such as *and* or *but*. The following quote is an example of good use of a semicolon.

> *Punctuation marks for this period [Middle Ages] seem to mean almost anything or almost nothing; in fact, punctuation for all authors of more than three or four centuries ago, and for most authors of two centuries ago, must be supplied by modern editors.*
> (From Charlton Laird, *The Miracle of Language*,
> Fawcett Publications, Greenwich, Conn., 1953, pp. 178–179.)

TIP: The semicolon is needed only in long, complex sentences, such as in the sample. You will not need it in most of your letter or report writing.

The *dash* (—) is sometimes used in place of a semicolon or as a stronger version of a comma to set off a phrase or clause.

TIP: If you are typing, a dash is made up of two hyphens.

EXAMPLE: To win the sweepstakes--and earn a bonus prize--mail your entry early.

The *colon* (:) is a pause that tells the reader something follows. The colon introduces material such as a long list or a quotation.

Most common use of the colon is in the salutation of business letters. (As discussed below you should use a comma in personal letters.)

EXAMPLES: Gentlemen: Dear Madam: Dear Editor:

Slight-Pause Punctuation

The *comma* (,) is the most frequently used internal mark. Deciding how to use it gives people hives. A comma indicates a slight pause. It also indicates relationship between words. Reading sentences out loud will give you a sense of their flow and will help you decide where to put commas.

Try to develop "comma sense" rather than trying to remember all the confusing rules, about which many experts disagree anyway. Apply the test of whether the comma's use helps convey your meaning.

A comma can change your meaning or make it more difficult for the reader to understand what you intend to communicate. Consider the following sentences:

EXAMPLE: After all it took him 10 hours to complete the job.
           After all, it took him 10 hours to complete the job.

In the sentence without the comma, the introductory phrase seems intended to modify or refer to all that it took him to do the job. In the sentence with the comma, "After all" is immediately understood to be an introductory exclamation. Although ultimately the meaning becomes clear, the sentence without the comma starts the reader off on the wrong foot.

Commas help make our language precise. Their presence or absence and position can cause subtle changes in meaning.

EXAMPLES: The computer, which crashed, is over there.
           The computer that crashed is over there.

The commas around "which crashed" tell the reader that the two words are not essential to the sentence's meaning and could be left out. The sentence says that there is only one computer and, incidentally, it crashed.

The sentence minus the commas tells the reader that the two

words are essential to the writer's message. More than one computer is around, but the one that crashed is the subject here.

The technical terms are *nonrestrictive* (doesn't affect the meaning) for the clause set off by the commas and *restrictive* (essential to the meaning) for the phrase without the commas.

FYI: Although "that" and "which" are used increasingly interchangeably, a rule exists: "That" introduces a restrictive clause; "which" introduces a nonrestrictive clause.

Here are other examples of how a comma can shift your meaning:

EXAMPLES: The light blue dress is in the closet.
The light, blue dress is in the closet.

After 10 days the clerk said I could return the merchandise if not satisfied.
After 10 days, the clerk said, I could return the merchandise if not satisfied.

In the first pair the subject of the sentence without a comma is a dress whose color is light blue. The second sentence, with the comma, is about a dress that is lightweight and is blue.

In the second pair, the sentence without the comma could mean that the clerk waited 10 days to tell me the merchandise could be returned. The commas make it clear that "After 10 days" is part of what the clerk told me, not when he or she said it. (Use of word order to clarify this sentence was discussed in Chapter 3.)

Commas often come in pairs. Leaving out the second comma can slightly shift your meaning. Writers most often forget the second comma when writing dates and addresses in a sentence.

Present We make pastries at the Groton, Connecticut, bakery.

Missing We make pastries at the Groton, Connecticut bakery.

Without the second comma after "Connecticut," the name of the state is separated from the town and joined to the bakery. The change suggests that Groton could be a Connecticut bakery and not the town in which the bakery is located. Although the grammar is wrong for this reading, there is still a chance that the reader will be confused, or at least distracted.

Present   A July 4, 1986, celebration marked the renovation of the Statue of Liberty.

Missing   A July 4, 1986 celebration marked the renovation of the Statue of Liberty.

Again, the missing second comma subtly changes the relationship of the words: 1986 is separated from July 4. "Celebration" appears to be modified by two different entities: something called a July 4 and something else called a 1986, otherwise unrelated to each other.

TIP: Commas often work in pairs, and if one of the partners is missing, the job is not done well.

Use the comma in the salutation of personal letters.

Dear Susan,   My Dear Husband,   Dear Bill,   Hi,

The Apostrophe

We use the apostrophe (') frequently. It is not a punctuation of pause. It performs two functions: (1) It indicates possession (e.g., *Dave's* toes) and (2) it indicates a missing letter (known as a *contraction: Don't* do that.)

The apostrophe causes problems only in a few situations. One such problem occurs with the word "it":

- Do *not* use the apostrophe to make "it" possessive.

- Do use an apostrophe when forming contractions with "it."

EXAMPLES: The dictionary was praised for *its* thoroughness.
It's time. (It is time.)

To form a possessive from a plural noun that ends in "s," add only an apostrophe, not a second "s." When the plural does not end in "s," add one after the apostrophe.

EXAMPLES: The teachers' skit was wonderful.
My brothers' bikes are ten-speeds.
The children's clothes looked lovely.
The people's reaction was subdued.

When forming a possessive from a name that ends in "s," you still should add the apostrophe and the second "s."

EXAMPLES: Mr. Davis's toes. (*Not:* Mr. Davis' toes.) Thomas's dissertation. (*Not:* Thomas' dissertation.)

Also, do not use the apostrophe with possessive pronouns.

EXAMPLES: The book is yours. (*Not:* The book is your's.) The decision is hers. (*Not:* The decision is her's.)

Never use an apostrophe to form plurals!

EXAMPLES: We sell fresh hot donuts. (*Not:* We sell fresh hot donut's.) How many books? (*Not:* How many book's?)

Miscellaneous Punctuation

You will occasionally need to use the following marks in your business or personal writing.

Asterisk (*) Use this rarely, if at all. Its most practical use in everyday writing is as a reference mark to refer to a note (footnote) at the bottom of the page or the end of the letter or article. When so used, put the asterisk at the end of the word or words connected to the reference and at the beginning of the note.

Hyphen (-). In many cases the use or nonuse of a hyphen is a matter of personal choice. The most common use in everyday writing is to mark the division of a word at the end of a line when the whole word will not fit. This, of course, requires knowing how to divide a word between syllables.

TIP: In general, don't divide words at the end of lines. Few words are so long that moving them to the next line will leave an undesirably short line.

Hyphens are used in compound words. Your choice with compound words is to write them as one word, two words, or with a hyphen. Check a dictionary if you are not certain. If the dictionary is not clear, use your own judgment. Just be sure to write the word the same way each time. Don't waste time on this sort of hyphen.

TIP: The trend is to use fewer hyphens. When in doubt, don't use one.

Hyphens can sometimes clarify the meaning of compound modifiers.

EXAMPLE: The light blue dress is in the closet.
The light, blue dress is in the closet.
The light-blue dress is in the closet.

The first sentence, with no internal punctuation, is unclear. The second sentence makes it clear that the dress is lightweight and blue. The third sentence uses the hyphen and makes it clear that the dress is light blue in color.

When compound modifiers come after the verb, the hyphen is not used.

EXAMPLE: The light-blue dress hangs in the closet.
The dress is light blue and hangs in the closet.

I have full-time work.
My work is full time.

Parentheses [( )]. If you want to add an aside, a bit of additional information, without changing the meaning of your sentence, put the addition in parentheses. Don't use this technique often. Parentheses always come in pairs: one at the beginning of the statement, its partner at the end.

EXAMPLE: Our condominiums, which are located near many recreational facilities (swimming, boating, golfing, horseback riding), are priced for middle-income families.

If you have a numbered or lettered list, you can use parentheses around the numbers or letters.

EXAMPLE: We all use four vocabularies: (1) speaking, (2) writing, (3) reading, and (4) recognition.

Some writers, particularly in business, put figures in parentheses immediately after writing the number in words.

EXAMPLE: You have thirty (30) days in which to pay.

Except when writing large numbers this practice wastes time and clutters the sentence. Use words or figures but not both unless the amount is very large and you wish to be certain it is clear. When writing a series of numbers, use figures only.

TIP: Generally, use words when writing numbers up through nine and figures for all higher numbers: one, two, three, etc.; 10, 11, 12, etc. At the beginning of a sentence write numbers as words: "Twelve persons make up a jury."

Quotation Marks (" ") always come in pairs, like parentheses. Don't forget the second one. Use them when you are quoting someone or something from another source. The quotation marks show that the words between them are not originating with you.

Put titles of books, magazines, articles, stories, movies, and poems within quotation marks.

FYI: Sometimes underlining is used instead of quotation marks for titles of magazines, books, and movies, but never for stories, articles, or poems.

Avoid the habit of putting quotation marks around ordinary words to suggest special meanings or around words to apologize for using them.

FYI: As a general rule, commas and periods are put inside the final quotation mark whether they go with the quoted material or not. Question and exclamation marks that belong with the quote go inside the final quotation mark. When a question or exclamation mark belongs to the sentence, however, it goes outside the final quotation mark.

TIP: Don't think about punctuation as you first write down your thoughts. Concentrate on what you want to say. When you have finished writing, go back, rewrite, and punctuate.

SPELLING MATTERS

Much as many of us might wish to ignore it, spelling is important. If you write "there" when you mean "their," you will blow a great big hole in your credibility, even if some meaning seeps through. Rightly or wrongly, readers do judge writers by their spelling and tend to decide that those who spell poorly are *not* worth reading.

At one time people did not pay any attention to spelling. But that was a long time ago, about when Chaucer was writing and changing spellings to fit rhymes. Today we have one correct way to spell each word (some words have two spellings, but even with these one spelling is preferred). We may accept different pronunciations, but not different spellings.

If a misspelled word does not turn your reader off, the flawed word will draw attention to itself and away from the message you are trying to convey.

The Only Spelling Rule

So spell correctly. A piece of easy advice, difficult to follow. English spelling is not always logical. Furthermore, there are no general rules you can rely on at all times. The only rule you can follow safely in spelling is

IF YOU DON'T KNOW, LOOK IT UP.

Troublesome Pairs

Several pairs of words in English have similar sounds and spelling and often confuse people. These words are not spelled exactly the same and do not mean the same thing. A few such words to be careful with:

Advice/Advise

Advice—a noun meaning information or a recommendation.

Examples: Buy low and sell high is good advice.
What investment advice can you give me?

Advise—a verb meaning to recommend or give advice.

Examples: We advise you to buy low and sell high.
My real estate broker advises me to accept the offer.

Affect/Effect

Affect—a verb meaning to influence, to change.

Examples: The weather affected the turnout for the game.
The high prices affected sales.

Affect—can also be a noun on rare occasions, but only in technical writing, such as in psychology.

Effect—most often used as a noun in everyday writing. It means result, or cause.

Examples: The weather had an effect on the turnout for the game.
The high prices had a bad effect on sales.
What was the effect of the sales campaign?

Effect—also a verb. As a verb it means to cause.

Examples: Reducing prices effected an increase in sales.
Customer protests effected a change in the company's warranty policy.

All Ready/Already

All ready—adjectival phrase meaning all prepared.

Examples: Your order is all ready to be shipped.
The unit is all ready to be installed.

Already—adverb meaning previously; by this time.

Examples: Your order has already been shipped.
The unit is already installed.

All Right/Alright

Alright—misspelling of all right. *Do not use.*

Appraise/Apprise

Appraise—a verb meaning to evaluate.

> *Examples:* Your house has been appraised at $150,000.
> Will you appraise my watch?

Apprise—a verb meaning to inform.

> *Examples:* Have you been apprised of our new low prices?
> Would you apprise me of my rights under the warranty?

TIP: Avoid "apprise." Use "inform."

Bad/Badly

Bad—an adjective modifying a noun.

> *Example:* It was a bad movie. I feel bad about the loss. (I am
sorry about it.)

Badly—an adverb modifying a verb.

> *Example:* The company suffered badly in the economic slump.

TIP: The "-ly" endings distinguish between adjectives, which modify nouns, and adverbs, which modify verbs. "I feel soft" expresses the condition of your body or muscles. "I feel softly" says that your touch is light.

Capital/Capitol

Capital—a noun meaning the seat of government.

> *Example:* Boston is the capital of Massachusetts.

Capital—also an adjective meaning first, foremost, excellent.

> *Example:* That is a capital idea.

NOTE: "Capital letters" are upper case letters: A, B, C, etc.

Capitol—noun meaning the building in which the legislature sits.

> *Example:* The capitol in Massachusetts has a golden dome.

Compose/Comprise

Compose—verb meaning to make up.

Example: Twenty articles compose the contract.

Comprise—verb meaning to consist of.

Example: The contract comprises 20 articles.

Good/Well

Good—an adjective.

Examples: The Compleat Computer provides good service.
At those prices, it was a good deal.
The coat of paint made the store look good.

Well—either an adverb or an adjective.

Examples: He did the repairs as well as he could. (Adverb.)
The company honored the warranty as well as any other company. (Adverb.)
Because of your product, I do not feel well. (Adjective.)

Imply/Infer

Imply—a verb meaning to suggest (what the speaker or writer does).

Example: The warranty implied free repair service.

Infer—a verb meaning to assume or deduce (what the listener or reader does).

Example: I inferred from the warranty that repair service was free.

Principal/Principle

Principal—a noun meaning a leading figure, a person acting on his or her own behalf, or, in a financial sense, capital or wealth either owned or owed.

Examples: She was principal of the high school.

He was the principal in the transaction.

He was paying only the interest and not the principal of the loan.

Her principal earned a high interest rate.

Principal—also an adjective indicating first, highest, foremost.

Examples: Poor service is the principal reason I am going to another garage.

Providing quality products at reasonable prices is our principal goal.

Principle—a noun meaning a basic truth or rule.

Examples: Checking your spelling in a dictionary is a sound principle to follow.

"The customer knows best" is the principle under which we operate.

Their/There

A hurrying and careless writer just might mix up these two words. Because their difference is so widely known, a writer who confuses the two will be quickly written off.

Their—a possessive pronoun, third person plural. In the sentence above, "their" refers to the two words in question.

Examples: According to their ad, the items were on sale.

I have hired their law firm to represent me.

There—an adverb indicating a point of action, time, or place. In everyday writing often used to introduce a sentence.

Examples: There are three cats in my backyard.

If there are any tickets left, please send me two.

There—a noun meaning a place.

Examples: Put the television set over there.

I want to go there for vacation.

Grammatical Booby Traps

Here are a few common grammatical errors to guard against.

Wrong   Between you and I

Right   Between you and me

Wrong   These sort, these kind, this here

Right   This sort, this kind, this

Wrong   Most unique (or any modifier with unique)

Right   Unique (means only one of a kind)

LEGIBILITY

You have accomplished nothing by writing if the recipient of your written message cannot read it. A rather obvious point, but one to keep in mind.

When you communicate in writing, you need to have everything possible going for you, and legibility is first among what is possible. It may be sad, but it is true, that a sloppy image can dull brilliant content. Neatness means a clean and orderly appearance.

You should be neat physically—appearance—and in the way you present your content—organization. (Chapters 1 and 3 cover organization of content.)

Writing by Hand

The wonders of this electronic age have not yet completely displaced the pen. Many people still feel that a personal letter should be handwritten. In the interest of legibility and speed, however, the typewriter and computer are perfectly acceptable for most personal letters.

TIP: One thing that is never acceptable is the *depersonalized* greeting card. The custom has grown, particularly among business people, to send Christmas greeting cards, for example, without a personally written signature. Their name is *printed* on the card along with the printed message. Actually, such a card delivers a very forceful message to the recipient; not, however, one the sender probably intended.

There are times when even the busy business executive must put pen to paper. In addition to signing her or his signature to a holiday greeting card (or at least having a secretary forge it), the executive should write notes of sympathy by hand. Notes of encouragement or of well-deserved congratulations warrant the hand-written word.

It is precisely at these times, when you want most to convey a sense of warmth, intimacy, and sincerity, that you must rely on your penmanship. Take pains with it. Print if you must. Do not at such times saddle the recipient of your message with the burden of deciphering it. You don't have to be a calligraphic artist; just have a good, clear hand.

When writing by hand, use a pen, not a pencil. It provides a clearer, sharper line and is much less likely to smudge and fade. Use a pen that won't smear or run if the paper gets wet. One with a relatively fine line works best. Except in personal correspondence, use neutral colors—blue or black. Avoid unusual eye-catching colors like purple or green, unless you intend to make a statement about yourself.

If you make a mistake, start over. Don't cross out the error. Sometimes you can get away with using a correcting fluid, but the fluid leaves a telltale mark. If you've gone out of your way to find the perfect birthday card, avoid unsightly blemishes on it by knowing what you want to say before you start writing.

If you do have to write to someone with a pencil, remember: soft lead, sharp point.

Writing with a Machine

A typewriter or computer printer nearly solves the problem of legibility. You must be careful to keep the keys clean and the ribbon new. And you must be sure to proofread everything, even after all your revisions and rewrites, to catch any typographical errors that may have crept in.

SUMMING UP

When you sit down to write, whatever you are writing, forget grammar, spelling, sentences, paragraphs. *Write*. Concentrate on what you want to say. Throw in the punctuation, make the sentences and paragraphs as they occur to you—right or wrong.

Write everything you want to say. Get in the detail. *Then* rewrite, and this time think about grammar, spelling, sentencing, paragraphing. Use these tools to make sure your reader gets the message.

To write effectively requires some effort, but you are capable of writing well and expressing your intended message clearly. Good writing is more the result of that extra rewrite than it is of some rare, inborn talent. Alexander Pope (1688–1744) put it rather well:

True ease in writing comes from art, not chance,
As those move easiest who have learn'd to dance.

SECTION TWO

LETTER ELEMENTS

Section Two examines the standard elements of letters and how subtle modifications of them affect your message. Some topics in this section may appear self-evident—everyone knows you date letters, have an opening greeting and a closing signature. Take some time with these topics anyway. They give your reader important clues, and each clue can help you write to the point.

There are different ways, for example, to write the date, and the way you write it can send a message about you. Your use of a comma or a colon in the salutation identifies your message as business or social. How do you address the person to whom you are writing? The wrong note in your greeting can turn off your reader. Do you always want to close with the same well-worn word, "Sincerely"?

You will find the elements arranged in the order in which they appear in a letter. Glance at each. You may learn different ways of using them to improve your message. Elements pertaining only to business writing are marked (B).

5

Letter Elements and Formats

All letters consist of the same basic elements. These are: return address (letterhead), date, interior address, attention line (B), salutation, subject line (B), body, complimentary close, name and/or signature, title, reference initials (B), enclosure (B), copy notation (B), postscript.

Few letters contain all these elements. Formal and business letters usually contain most of them, including attention and subject lines that will never appear in social or personal letters. A postscript is optional but, as you will read below, rather than serving as an afterthought, a postscript can play a prominent role.

RETURN ADDRESS (LETTERHEAD)

This is your address. It appears at the very top of the letter, either in the left corner, center, or right corner. (See the material on business letter formats at the end of this chapter.) Usually it uses separate lines for your name, street address, and city, state, and zip code, but it can be one long line across the top of the paper. On business letters the return address should contain your telephone number. On social and personal letters the telephone number is optional and is usually left off. Wherever you put it, be sure that your mailing address is complete.

Tɪᴘ: Some writers today put the return address at the end of the letter. Even on a 1-page letter this practice makes the curious reader look around to see where the letter is coming from. Be up front with your readers; don't make them work unnecessarily. Put your return address at the top.

When writing a personal letter, you may decide not to include your return address. That's fine in some circumstances. Leaving it out says you are on close enough terms with the person receiving your letter that she or he knows what your address is. In such a situation, your writing it on your letter actually distances you from the reader and wastes everyone's time.

Never leave your return address out of your letter on the grounds that your reader can get it off the envelope. Envelopes have a way of getting torn apart, dropped into wastebaskets, or being used for scrap paper.

The standard positions for return address information are illustrated below and on the opposite page.

Vivian Vital
1234 Main Street
Anywhere, Ohio 11111

Vivian Vital
1234 Main Street
Anywhere, Ohio 11111

Vivian Vital, 1234 Main Street, Anywhere, Ohio 11111

TIP: The custom today is to leave out the comma at the end of each line of the address. The only punctuation marks in addresses listed by lines are the comma between the community and the state and a period after some abbreviations.

Abbreviate or Not?

You face one of your first questions of style when writing your address. The choice you make should be reflected throughout your letter. Avoid mixing styles. Either abbreviate or do not abbreviate throughout.

TIP: *Never* put a comma between the name of the state, whether spelled out or abbreviated, and the zip code.

In the sample shown, abbreviations were not used. Note that the word "street" was spelled out and so was the name of the state. Generally, words that can customarily be abbreviated should either all be written in full or all be shortened—whatever you decide. If you use "St." or "Ave.," abbreviate the name of the state. Do not write out "Street" and then use the abbreviation "rm." for "room."

TIP: Compass designations in addresses that follow a street name and indicate a section or area are *always* abbreviated: 999 16th Avenue NW, Atlanta, Georgia. The District of Columbia is also always abbreviated as D.C. or DC.

A growing custom is to use the U.S. Post Office designations for states even if other words, such as "street," and "avenue," are spelled out. This is particularly evident in business writing, in which a desire to project an image of speed and efficiency sometimes outweighs the desire to have a consistent style.

TIP: If you do use the Post Office designations for states, write them with two capital letters and no period.

In business letters, your name and title are usually included in the return address. In personal or social letters they usually are not. There is no hard and fast rule on this. Do what seems sensible and what you prefer. (See "Complimentary Close" below.)

Printed Letterheads

Most businesses use printed letterheads that carry the name of the business, its address, and, usually, its telephone number. Company officers often have printed letterheads that also include their own name and title.

Many individuals also have printed letterheads for their personal correspondence. This is a perfectly acceptable practice for all kinds of personal letter writing. Such letterhead is a timesaver, and a strikingly printed letterhead conveys a message about the writer.

DATE

Always date everything you write: letters, memos, notes, reports, minutes. Put down the *full* date: day, month, and year. Don't forget the year! Writing the date takes about two seconds. Trying to remember when you wrote something can take forever.

Impersonal letters prepared by computers and mailed to several thousand people often carry no date or only a partial date. Most of these letters go right into the wastebasket. Don't computerize your important messages. Your letter will stimulate action and probably be filed, so the date is crucial.

The date appears on the top of your letter. If you use a return address, the date is the second item, coming right after and just below your address. If you do not use a return address, the date is the first item to appear. It can be flush left (against the left margin), centered, or flush right (ending against the right margin). (See "Business Letter Formats" at the end of this chapter.)

TIP: Putting the date against the right margin at or near the top (flush right) is the common practice. In this position the date can be easily seen, which expedites filing.

It's Practical and Courteous

The date serves a practical purpose of expediting your message as well as being a courtesy. If you have put the full date at the top of your letter, you do not need to resort to using specific dates and day names in the text. You can use phrases that are natural and flow freely, such as "last week," "yesterday," "this coming weekend." Your reader has already seen or need only glance at the date at the top to know exactly what you mean.

Of course, if you are setting up an appointment, you should write the exact date *and* time in the text.

Tip: In a personal letter to a friend or relative, add the name of the day to the date. Such a touch can heighten the sense of intimacy or sharing such a letter should convey. January 1, 2000, gives the exact day, certainly, but most people would have to look at a calendar to know that this is a Monday. By adding the name of the day to the date at the top, it helps your reader imagine you on that particular day, and perhaps think back to what he or she may have been doing.

In business correspondence, especially if there is any likelihood that there will be follow-up letters, dating letters is essential. Many companies file letters by date as well as by subject matter.

Formats for Dates

You can write the date in several ways. Use the one that fits the image you want your message to convey.

Traditional

In the United States, we traditionally write the date in the order month-day-year, with the name of the month spelled out and with a comma between the date of the month and the year:

>   January 27, 1990

You cannot go wrong using this format.

European

In Europe the custom is to write the date in the order day-month-year, with the month's name spelled out and with *no* comma:

>   27 January 1990

This format has been gaining favor in the United States, and some feel that it has a modern, businesslike image. If you think so and wish to convey such an image, use this format. If you do use this format, *do not* put a comma between the month and year. Such a gaffe mars your image.

Breezy

Whichever format—traditional or European—you select, you can write the date in all numbers:

> 1/27/90   or   27/1/90

This is the abbreviated version of the date and you would *not* use it in a letter in which you were not using the abbreviated style.

Use this style on memos, short notes, or informal letters in which you want to convey a sense of haste or urgency.

INTERIOR ADDRESS

The interior address should be the same as the one you use on the envelope. The interior address includes the following (in order):

- Name of the person to whom you write with appropriate courtesy or professional title
- Business title (if any)
- Division or branch (if any)
- Company name (if any)
- Address

Titles

There are three kinds of titles a person can possess:

1. Courtesy (e.g., Mrs., Ms., Miss, Mr.),
2. Professional (e.g., Dr., Governor, Professor), and

3. Business (e.g., President, General Manager, Treasurer).

TIP: Courtesy and professional titles always appear *before* the name. Business titles always appear *after* the name. Never use business titles in the salutation. (See "Salutation" and "What Title to Use?" below.)

When and Where to Use an Interior Address

The interior address should always appear on all business correspondence as well as on formal social correspondence. It is optional, if not out of place, on informal and personal letters.

The interior address goes against the left margin (flush left), with a space between it and the date line. Follow the style you decided on in writing your return address—abbreviated or written out. Use the same punctuation or lack thereof.

TIP: On formal social correspondence and on letters that are a mix of business and social, the interior address is often placed at the end of the letter, about five lines below the name and title, still flush left.

Use the person's full name and title in the interior address, regardless of how you will greet the individual in the salutation and body of the letter. Be certain that you spell the name correctly and have the right title. There is no bigger turnoff than a misspelled name or an incorrect title. Many people who receive mail with their name misspelled throw the unread letter into the wastebasket or at best read it with a bias. And those who have worked hard for a professional title like to see it used.

If you are writing to an organization and cannot find the name of an individual to address, use only a title in the address. ("President" is always a good one when in doubt, or "Public Affairs Officer" in a large organization.) If you cannot think of an appropriate title, just begin with the company name. (See "Salutation," below.)

ATTENTION LINE (B)

On business letters only, and not really necessary there, the *attention line* stresses the business character over the personal character of the letter. By using it you say that anyone acting for the person as well as the person indicated on the attention line can open and respond to your letter.

Since the only other purpose of the attention line is to direct your letter to the right person or department, which can as easily and more naturally be done by including the necessary information in the address itself—both on the envelope and interior address—you can leave it out. Today all letters addressed to businesses and individuals in business, unless otherwise marked, are considered business letters. Thus you do not need to use the attention line to achieve this purpose.

What you need do if you *are* sending a personal letter to an organization and want only the particular individual to open it is to write the word "Personal" on the envelope. "Confidential," "Personal and Private," any word or phrase will do to indicate the nature of your letter. If you want to stress the point, you can also write "Personal" at the top of the letter itself, centered below the letterhead or above a typed return address.

If you use an attention line, it should appear a double space below the interior address on the letter. The salutation comes a double space below it. On the envelope, the attention line can be included in the address after the name of the organization or just below and to the right of the address, which is better because it stands out more clearly.

If you want to indicate a personal letter, the word "Personal," or whichever word you select, should appear prominently below and to the right or left of the address on the envelope.

SALUTATION

With the salutation—"Dear..."—you speak directly to the recipient of your letter for the first time. This greeting should strive for the right note, but your major practical aim is to avoid striking the wrong note.

You can hardly go wrong starting with the tried and true "Dear..." But directly after that you must use an individual's most precious possessions—name and title. The salutation offers unwary writers many ways to insult the recipients of their letters: a misspelled name, an incorrect title, an unwarranted familiarity.

No Salutation (B)

The salutation is disappearing from business letters, and using no salutation is one way to avoid the booby traps in this simple line, although some sensitive souls might be slightly insulted by the absence of the salutation. Those who advocate doing away with the salutation in business correspondence argue that it has become stilted and meaningless. And everyone—writer, typist, reader—saves time when the line is omitted, so that not using it can appear to be a symbol of efficiency and modernity for a "go-go" company in a frenetic society. But do not reject it lightly.

Salutation Punctuation

Punctuating the salutation line is easy. Just remember these two rules and the one exception:

1. In business correspondence use a colon at the end: Dear Ms. Smith:

2. In personal and social letters use a comma at the end: Dear Arnold,

EXCEPTION: Sometimes in personal letters with informal salutations, an exclamation point is used in place of the comma: Hi!

The only other punctuation in the salutation line will be the period after abbreviations, such as in titles.

What Title To Use?

Mr., Mister, Miss, Mrs., Ms., Dr.? If writing to a personal friend, no title is used in the salutation—no problem. In business or formal social writing, if you know what the person prefers (as indicated, for example, by a letter from the person), no problem. Otherwise, especially when writing to women in business, you have a problem: Is she married, single, modern, conservative?

Use the professional title if you know it: Dr., Professor, Senator. Do *not* use a person's business rank or position in the salutation:

No   Dear Personnel Manager Wool:

No   Dear Ms. Wool, Personnel Manager:

Yes   Dear Ms. Wool:

When in doubt about how a woman prefers to be addressed, simply leave out the title (*and* the "dear"):

> Harriet White: (See "Full Name? Last Name? First Name? Nickname?" page 97.)

or use the neutral "Ms.":

> Dear Ms. White:

Tip: Abbreviate Mr., Mrs., Ms., and Dr. in the salutation. Also Messrs. (Messieurs) is used to address more than one man in the salutation as:

> Dear Messrs. White, Brown, and Jones

Do *not* abbreviate any other titles you use in the salutation.

"Miss," of course, is not an abbreviation, so do not mistakenly put a period with it.

Other than "Dear"

The use of the word "Dear" in the salutation is a long-standing convention. Some people, though, feel awkward about using it. Some are bored with it.

Business

In business you have three acceptable alternatives regarding the use of "Dear" in the salutation: (1) leave out the salutation altogether,

(2) leave out the "Dear" and use only the professional title and name, (3) add the word "My" as in My dear Ms. White or My dear Juan: (actually considered more formal).

TIP: Do *not* capitalize "dear" unless it is the first word in the salutation.

Social

In social correspondence you have only two choices: (1) the standard Dear Mrs. Hendle or Dear Joan, or (2) My dear Dr. Gomez, My dear George.

Personal

In personal, informal correspondence, you have a wide range of choices ranging from leaving out the "Dear" to emphasizing it:

> My darling Rosita (or wife, lover, sweetheart)
> My dearest Carl (or husband, lover, friend)

Let yourself go, use your imagination. If uncertain of the tone you want to strike, however, stay with the standard "Dear." But your salutation can be intimate, warm, friendly, breezy, offhand, or just about what you want it to be. For instance, use the "Dear" with a descriptive name to liven up the greeting and strike a certain note:

> Dear Friend, Dear Pal, Dear Husband, Dear Wife

Some other ideas include:

Hi, or Hello, (with or without a name)

What's Up? (using a question mark instead of a comma)

Good Day! (using an exclamation point instead of a comma)

Ciao! (Italian for Hi!, Hello!, or So long!) (See discussion of *complimentary close* in "Personal Breezy," below.)

TIP: You can use in your salutation just about any greeting people use when meeting each other. Avoid, however, the word "Greetings" by itself. It calls to mind that draft boards used it when notifying individuals called up for service in the armed forces. Thus, it may for some have lost a certain warmth.

Full Name? Last Name? First Name? Nickname?

How you use a person's name in the salutation depends on how well you know the person. If you are answering a letter, you can take your cue from how the person signed the letter. In general, however, follow the safe rule:

DO NOT PRESUME.

If you are not sure whether William White prefers William, Will, Bill, Billy, or Willie, your best choice is Dear Mr. White; your second best is Dear William.

If uncertain of the preferred title, use the last name (surname) with the professional or courtesy title:

Dear Ms. Williams,   Dear Professor Knickman:

Another possibility is to use the full name *without* "Dear":

William White:

TIP: Some people use "dear" with the full name. Some even feel that such use conveys a special warmth. On the contrary, it advertises the fact that you are uncertain how to address the person, that you are not close enough to use the first name, and that you don't know the preferred title. Computers use this form of salutation. People, even those using a computer, do not.

To Persons Unknown

Sometimes you must write a letter to a company or organization, and, despite efforts to find out, you do not have an individual's name or know which particular official to address. Use the salutations shown below. Generally avoid the "Dear." When writing to all-male organizations:

Gentlemen: Sirs: Dear Sirs:

When writing to all-female organizations:

Ladies: Mesdames: (French and formal)

When writing to organizations of females and males:

Ladies and Gentlemen:

TIP: Although "Gentlemen" alone has the sanction of years of use
for addressing organizations of mixed sexes, beginning in the
1960s in the United States such usage began to lose favor on the
grounds that it slighted women. It does. Avoid it.

To avoid sexist traps and strike a less formal note, use:

Friends:

If you do not feel particularly friendly toward the organization, use
the coolly formal:

To whom it may concern:

Another informal approach you can take is to use the company's
name in the salutation:

Dear IBM: Dear AT&T: Dear Exxon:

Sometimes you know the official's title, but not the name. Don't
forget, if writing to an organization and you want some action, it
is not a bad idea to address your letter to the president or chief
executive officer. Do not, however, use such a title in the salutation.

If you do not have a name, use the singular of appropriate salutations noted above, such as:

Madam: Sir: Friend: (with or without "Dear")

Double Salutations

The need can arise to write a letter addressed to two individuals,
especially in social writing. If you are writing two individuals associated professionally, no problem exists. Put both names (titles if

any) in the address (on both the envelope and interior address) and in the salutation:

Dear Ms. McGarry and Dr. Weaver,

Writing to couples requires a little more thought, because several possibilities exist and selecting the wrong one can alienate one or both individuals with whom you wish to communicate. Below are some of the possible relationships you will encounter and the right way to address each.

Married Couple, Traditional

Dear Mr. and Mrs. Olsen,

On the envelope and interior address put

Mr. and Mrs. Otto T. Olsen

Married Couples with Titles

Often one or both spouses holds a professional title. In such a case, use the title. If both have titles:

Dear Professor and Dr. Williams,

On the envelope and interior address use the following

Professor John Williams
Dr. Elizabeth Williams

If one has a title:

Dear Governor and Mr. Graziano, (wife's title)
Dear Dr. and Mrs. Lopez, (husband's title)

On the envelope and interior address, if the husband has a title:

Dr. and Mrs. Juan Lopez

If wife has a title, use:

Governor Ella Graziano
Mr. John Graziano

Married Couple Maiden Name

Sometimes a woman retains her maiden name after marriage. In this case, use both names and appropriate professional titles on the envelope, interior address, and in the salutation.

Unmarried Couple

As with a married couple in which the woman retains her maiden name, use both names and appropriate professional titles on the envelope, interior address, and in the salutation.

SUBJECT LINE (B)

The *subject line* is used only in business correspondence, but this includes letters from an individual to a business (seeking a job, seeking a refund, making a complaint) as well as letters from business to business. All internal memos carry a subject line. The line quickly informs the reader of the topic and also helps with filing.

TIP: The subject line sometimes replaces the salutation on business letters.

The subject line appears an extra space below the salutation with another space between it and the body of the letter. You can either center it or keep it flush against the left margin. If flush left, begin it with the word "Subject:"

TIP: If you center the subject line, leave out the word "Subject:" You need the word "subject" if the line is flush left to make it clear that this is not the first sentence of the body of the letter.

In place of "Subject" you can use "In re:" or just "Re:" "In re" is a Latin phrase meaning in the matter of or concerning, although some mistakenly take it to be an abbreviation for in regard to.

Capitalize all the major words of a subject line. For special emphasis put the line in all capitals or underline it. If you do use all capitals or an underline, you do not need to use "Subject," or "In re," or "Re."

Some people avoid using all capitals because words in all capitals are harder to read. That, however, is hardly a major consideration for a line that will rarely, if ever, exceed four or five words. If your subject line runs longer than five words, you reduce its effectiveness anyway as a quick identification of your topic.

BODY

The body of your letter—your message—is its most important part and the focus of this book. The first six chapters give you fundamental writing skills. Subsequent chapters give you many examples of those skills applied in concrete situations.

COMPLIMENTARY CLOSE

When you finish a face-to-face conversation, you do not simply turn and walk away. When you finish a telephone conversation, you do not simply hang up. In both situations, if only to avoid appearing rude, you say, "Good-bye," "So long," "Thanks," "See you," or some such phrase. So it is with letters. When you finish conveying your message, you end it gracefully with a *complimentary close*.

You have many style and wording choices for your complimentary close. It can be formal traditional, informal traditional, personal, intimate, cool, warm, breezy, modern. As with the salutation, your complimentary close should reflect your relationship to your reader. The same style should be followed in both. If in the salutation you used the formal, impersonal, cool "Dear Sir," you should not use an informal, personal, warm complimentary close such as "All the best."

TIP: Only the first letter of the complimentary close is capitalized. The line ends with a comma.

No Complimentary Close (B)

Although it serves to avoid the appearance of impersonal abruptness, not to say rudeness, the complimentary close is often left off business letters. The rationale for discarding the convention is that the same words—"sincerely," "yours truly," "respectfully"—have been used to the point where they have lost all meaning and any sense of personal warmth. Thus, the reasoning goes, they add nothing and waste time, so forget them.

Routine, impersonal business letters, especially ones that are essentially form letters, do not need the complimentary close. *Always,* however, include a complimentary close on any letter that is at all personal, and many business letters can—and should—be personal. If you do not use the complimentary close, simply put your name after the body of your letter. (See discussion of Name and Signature below.)

Some Complimentary Closes

Any expression you use when ending a conversation can be used in the complimentary close. Custom, however, has standardized certain phrases, which are perfectly acceptable, cover most situations, and are frequently used. Do try to personalize your complimentary close and strive for originality, but when in doubt, rely on custom. Below are conventional and nonconventional samples arranged in categories that suggest the situation in which to use them.

Formal Traditional Closes

These complimentary closing lines are quite formal and suitable for business or social letters. The ones in the left column are those most often used.

Very truly yours,	Very respectfully yours,
Very sincerely yours,	Respectfully yours,
Very cordially yours,	Respectfully,

For variation, you can put "yours" at the beginning of the line instead of at the end:

Yours very truly,	Yours very respectfully,
Yours very sincerely,	Yours respectfully,
Yours very cordially,	

Informal Traditional Closes

These traditional closings are less formal and more personal. They are suitable for business, social, or personal letters.

Sincerely,   Sincerely yours,

Cordially,   Cordially yours,

Yours truly,

Informal Personalized Closes

When writing to someone you do not know personally, use a traditional complimentary close, but when writing—even a business letter—to someone you *do* know, try to avoid the traditional. Personalize your complimentary close. Some suggestions:

Best wishes,   Regards,

Warmest regards,   Warmly,

Best regards,   All the best,

Thanks,   Thanks for your help,

Thank you,   Thank you for helping,

Merry Christmas,   Happy New Year,

Best wishes of the   Happy holiday,
season,

Good luck!   With all good wishes,

With best wishes to
you and your (wife
or husband),

Personal and Warm

In a personal letter, you can tailor the complimentary close as you wish. Any of the traditional closes are acceptable, except those that are stiffly formal. You may adopt a particular close as your own trademark for use with friends. Below find some suggestions with comments.

Love,   (used so much as to have
become a convention)

With love, I love you,	(and other variations to be used only if such emphasis is intended)
Your loving (wife/ husband/ friend/etc.),	
Your (loving/ affectionate/close) friend,	
Congratulations!	(as appropriate)
Condolences,	(as appropriate)
With sympathy,	(as appropriate)
With affection,	
Yours in peace,	
As ever,	

Personal and Breezy

Acquaintances, friends who have a good relationship but prefer not to use a complimentary close that expresses affection, have a wide range of phrases from which to select. Depending on the relationship and message, just about any catchy concluding phrase can be used.

Auf Wiedersehen,	(German for "till we meet again"—note capitalization)
Au revoir,	(French for "till we meet again")
Cheers,	
Ciao!	(Italian for "So long")
Hang in there,	
Keep fighting,	
Keep the faith,	
Sayonara!	(Japanese for "Good-bye!")
See ya,	

So long,

Ta ta,   (Britishism for "So long")

Take it easy,

Your colleague,

Your friend,

Yours,

NAME AND SIGNATURE

Sign your letters in the way you wish the person you are writing to address you. On business and formal social letters that are typewritten, your *full* name should also be typewritten. You sign it as you wish the person to address you:

Written signature:

Typed name: N. Thomas Smith.

If your name appears in a letterhead, do *not* type it again at the end of the letter. Simply sign it.

On personal letters, even those you type, do *not* type your name. Simply sign the letter as you wish the person to address you.

Professional Titles

If you wish to be addressed by your professional title, include it in the typed version of your name. Put it after your name:

Betty Sawyer, Ph.D   John T. Smith, M.D.

Olin Burgess, Professor   Mildred White, Colonel,
                                      USA

In the top two examples, the person would be addressed as "Dr." If the academic initials do not indicate your correct professional title, then you put the title before your name:

Rev. Cotton Mather

Business Titles

Your business title should appear after your typed name on a line below it on all business correspondence. If your name and title appear in the letterhead, you do not need to repeat either where you sign the letter.

TIP: Leave your business title off all social and personal letters.

Courtesy Titles

A man does not need either to type or to sign the courtesy title "Mr." unless his name is one of those that could apply to either gender. If "Mr." is used, either type it or sign it, but do not do both. If signing, put it in parentheses.

A woman should use the courtesy title by which she wishes to be addressed. Whatever title is used—Miss, Ms., Mrs.,—either type it or sign it, but do not do both. If signing, put it in parentheses.

REFERENCE INITIALS (B)

On business correspondence, it is customary to type the initials of the writer (usually in capitals) followed by a colon and the initials of the typist (usually in lower case letters) at the left margin, two lines below the signature.

The initials of the writer are really superfluous on this line and can be left out. The initials of the typist serve to identify quickly the person who typed the letter: to place blame if an error has been made, to praise otherwise. Typists who are proud of their skill no doubt favor the custom.

ENCLOSURES (B)

The enclosure line at the bottom of the letter notes that additional material has been sent. It can be used to indicate exactly what the material is. It serves as a quick checklist for both the sender and receiver. If additional material is being sent separately, it can be used to convey that information as well.

The enclosure line is found almost exclusively on business correspondence. A private individual might have occasion to send an enclosure with a letter to a friend, business, or lawyer, in which case the form should be used.

The enclosure line starts at the left margin just below the reference initials or a line space below the name. It can take several forms, either abbreviated or spelled out. Keep it simple:

Enc.

Enc. (2) [or whatever number]

Check [or Invoice or whatever] enclosed

If you are sending the matter separately, indicate so on this line:

Sep. cov. Sweater [or whatever is being sent]

COPY NOTATIONS (B)

Copy notation is exclusively a business correspondence element, a not-so-innocent line that can spur action, raise hackles, or incite pleasure. It is a line that informs the receiver that you are sending copies of your message to another party or parties. It can be a courtesy; it can be a club. A little line with a lot of clout.

For example, if you write to a company seeking redress for shoddy service or merchandise, a notation that a copy of the letter is heading to the Better Business Bureau or other appropriate regulatory agency often does much to stimulate the desired reaction.

Noting that you are sending a copy of a complaint and request for corrective action to an individual's superior, however, could have an adverse affect, putting your receiver in a defensive position more eager to justify prior actions than to satisfy you. On the other hand, a notation that a copy of a complimentary message is being sent to an individual's superior or persons of influence adds impact to your praise, cementing a relationship and creating a receptive mind for future communications.

The copy notation begins at the left margin on the next line below the last previous element, whichever it is (name, reference initials, enc.). Use this form:

c: Name

The initials "cc" for carbon copy are commonly used, but why bother typing the extra "c," and, besides, today more copies come from duplicating machines and are not carbons. So be brief and be accurate. The name can be the name of a person or organization. If it's a person, use the full name and title, if any. If copies are going to more than one person, list them in order of importance or, to be safe, alphabetically. Enclosures rarely are sent to the individual(s) receiving copies. If enclosures are sent, the notation should read:

c/enc: Name

In some business situations, it may seem best to forgo the courtesy of informing the primary receiver that a copy of the message is being sent to others. This is known as a "blind copy," and some might question the ethics of the practice. When sending a blind copy, the notation appears only on the copies, not on the original, so you will know what you have done, but the receiver will not.

The notation follows the form used for regular copies with a "b" added:

bcc: or bc:

Do not put this notation at the bottom of the letter, however, but at the top left corner of the copies, so you or your secretary can spot it quickly in the file. Make sure you never mistakenly mark the original "bc"—it could create problems for you!

POSTSCRIPT

You can pack a lot of punch in a postscript. But it will be just a wild swing if you use it for an afterthought or an important fact you failed to include in the body of your message. Better to rewrite the letter than convey the impression of being disorganized.

So, despite the postscript's reputation as a place for an after-thought, give it forethought; use its eye-catching position to close with an emphatic impact. Deliberately withhold an idea for the post-script.

TIP: Write your postscript by hand for additional wallop. A hand-written note on the bottom of a typed letter calls out for atten-tion and conveys a personal touch to the reader.

Put the postscript a double space below the last previous ele-ment in the letter, at the left margin. If paragraphs are indented, indent the first line of the postscript also. Begin it with the initials "PS" followed by either a comma or a colon. The initials "PS" are always capitalized.

You can present a second idea in an additional postscript, as a separate paragraph that you label with the initials "PPS" (post-postscript) followed by a period or colon. Don't make the common mistake of writing "PSS."

Keep postscripts brief: one or two short sentences. Don't write a whole new letter in the postscript.

BUSINESS LETTER FORMATS

Business letter formats—margins, indents, spacing, and, to some extent, punctuation—occur in four common styles: *Block, modified* (or *semi-*) *block, modified* (or *semi-*) *block with indented paragraphs,* and *simplified* (*open*). Using a standard format makes it easier to prepare a neat, professional-looking letter. Never mix different styles within one letter.

Block Style

All elements start against the left margin (flush left). Only tables, quotations, or similar material within the body of the text are in-dented.

LETTERHEAD

Return Address
(If no letterhead)
_____

Date

Internal Address
_____

_____

Dear _____ :

_____

_____

_____

_____

_____ .

_____

_____

_____ .

_____

——————— Quotation ———————

_____

_____

_____

_____ .

Sincerely,

Name
Title

Reference Initials
Enclosures
cc:

Modified Block Style

The modified block style is possibly the most commonly used format in business letters. It is just like the block style with these exceptions: The return address (if no letterhead), date, and complimentary closing with name/title all start at the center point.

LETTERHEAD

Return Address
(If no letterhead)

_____

Date

Internal Address

_____

_____

Dear _____ :

_____
_____
_____
_____
_____ .

_____
_____
_____ .

_____
_____
_____ .

Sincerely,

Name
Title

Reference Initials
Enclosures
cc:

Modified Block Style with Indented Paragraphs

This style is like the modified block style with this exception: The first line of each paragraph is indented 5 spaces.

LETTERHEAD

Return Address
(If no letterhead)
_____

Date

Internal Address
_____
_____

Dear _____ :

    _____
_____
_____
_____
_____ .

_____
_____ .

    _____
_____
_____ .

Sincerely,

Name
Title

Reference Initials
Enclosures
cc:

Simplified Style

This is a newer style than the others. It eliminates the salutation and the complimentary close and uses open punctuation. Some feel it has a cold, brusque appearance. Those who like it feel it has a streamlined, no-nonsense, businesslike appearance.

A subject line replaces the salutation. Open punctuation means no punctuation at the end of any lines outside the body of the letter. At the close of the letter, the writer's name and title appear on one line, in all capitals. Other than these exceptions, the simplified style uses the block style format, in that all lines begin at the left margin.

LETTERHEAD

Return Address
(If no letterhead)
_____
Date

Internal Address
_____
_____

SUBJECT LINE

_____

_____

_____

_____

_____ .

_____

_____

_____ .

—————— Quotation ——————

——————————————————————————————

——————————————————————————————

——————— .

Name, Title

Reference Initials
Enclosures
cc:

SUMMING UP

The basic elements of a letter have added up to an imposing number of pages. Don't be overwhelmed. The chapter covers everything
you will ever need to know about letter elements. No, we are not
going to add "but were afraid to ask." On the contrary, don't be
afraid to ask. That is, if you have a question about an element when
writing a letter, look it up. Ignore whatever you do not need. The
information will be there when you need it.

SECTION THREE

EFFECTIVE WRITING AT WORK

Previous sections gave you the fundamentals necessary to develop good writing skills, skills that apply to any kind of writing. In this section and the next, you will find good and bad examples of specific kinds of writing, along with additional tips and insights particular to a specific category. The categories of samples were selected to represent typical writing goals.

This section examines samples of typical business writing. It identifies common pitfalls to avoid, as well as more effective ways to write to the point. It also covers matters of etiquette and protocol.

With the proliferation of computers, many business people now have word processors capable of correcting spelling, checking syntax, and formatting automatically. Given this powerful technology, a natural question is whether one really needs to develop writing skills. The answer is yes—a paradox of our time is that these electronic writing aids have *increased* the need for writing skills. Computers make it so easy to put words on paper, to manipulate those words, and to print out many copies. They do not, however, establish the quality of the writing, except in a rudimentary way. The quality of the writing still rests on the writer's skill. If you have not developed writing skills, the computer's power will expose your shortcomings to more people more quickly.

6

Typical Business Letters

The ultimate tool of business is the letter. The tools of production—lathes, drill presses, welding torches—are essential, as are the tools of service—computers, file cabinets, telephones. Ultimately, however, all organizations must resort to the written word, usually in a letter, sometimes in a memo or report, to carry out business.

Probably the major purpose of all business writing is to persuade or sell. Whatever other purpose it may have, such as providing or seeking information, the underlying purpose of any good business letter is to persuade the reader to use the products or services that business provides. That means retaining the reader's goodwill. In a few extreme cases, the business may no longer desire the reader's goodwill and future custom. Usually, however, even when refusing credit or seeking an overdue payment, retaining goodwill is a prime consideration.

The sample letters below are arranged, somewhat arbitrarily, into subject categories so that you can quickly find a letter that suits a particular need. Elements such as date, return address, internal address, and complimentary close are shown only if necessary to illustrate a point.

Tip: Always make the date on your letter the date of mailing. Usually it is, but sometimes in a busy office, especially when letters are typed in a typing pool, there is a 1- or 2-day delay before mailing. In such cases the origination date is 1 or 2 days earlier than the postmark. A relatively minor point, but some people do look at postmarks. A letter with an earlier date than the post-mark indicates that it sat around the office for a while before being mailed. This apparent lack of interest or enthusiasm can infect the reader. Avoid it. If you are preparing a letter late in the day, use the next day's date, because that is when it will probably be mailed. Some word processing programs have a com-mand that allows you to specify the date the letter is printed out, rather than the date it is written. Usually the letter is mailed on the day it is printed out.

PROVIDING INFORMATION

Although a good business letter focuses on one subject or purpose, it must always serve a dual purpose. It can simultaneously provide information and persuade the reader to use a service. The samples below provide information in a variety of contexts.

Dear Mr. Samuels:

In response to our telephone conversation this morning, I be-lieve your concern about entering into an hourly time and materials contract was well-founded. To give you a better sense of what the work will cost, I have developed a flat daily rate as follows.

Green Tree & Landscape will furnish three workers a day (a day being 8 to 10 hours per worker) for the purpose of pro-viding land-clearing services as discussed in our last proposal. Inclusive in our daily rate: all machinery needed to perform the work.

Daily flat rate $720.00

I have based our rates on the assumption that we will be working on site for approximately two weeks and in consid-eration of possible future work. You may, however, cancel this contract at any time and for any reason.

I am sure you will be pleased with our work. I look forward to hearing from you.

CRITIQUE: Basically a good letter addressing a potential customer's concern. A few minor changes would improve it. In the second paragraph, first sentence, the phrase "for the purpose of providing" could be shortened to "to provide." In the last sentence in that paragraph, the phrase "Inclusive in our daily rate" could be improved to "Our daily rate includes." Less pompous, more direct. In general, when writing dollar amounts do not bother with the decimal and zeros (unless, of course, the amount gives actual cents): $720 instead of $720.00.

Dear Ms. Ethelrod:

Your letter of January 2 to Mr. Goldberg has been passed to me for reply.

In view of the circumstances related in your letter, we are willing to return the copyright on *Indigenous Flora of Central Borneo* to the authors and enclose the appropriate documents for execution. We have also declared the book out-of-print and will destroy the remaining stock on hand.

I trust that these steps meet with your approval and that you will contact me if I can be of further assistance.

CRITIQUE: This is a direct, to-the-point letter that in three concise paragraphs establishes the reason for writing, covers the essential points, encourages approval, and offers further assistance.

Dear Samantha:

I have finalized my plans for attending the EBS Sales Conference. I will be there on Monday morning and will also try to sit in on the CUE Discussion on Wednesday, January 7, at 9:30 a.m.

Since CUE will be on our minds, it might make sense for us to get together in Tarrytown after the closing remarks. Perhaps we could talk over lunch at the hotel.

As an alternative, I plan to be in the New York office on Thursday morning, January 8, meeting with Betty Kaplow.

If this day would be more convenient for you, I'm sure we can arrange a time to get together.

I will give you a call from Tarrytown on Monday morning to check your schedule and see what's best for you.

Hope you had a nice holiday. I look forward to seeing you soon.

CRITIQUE: Effective letter, sharing information and making arrangements for a meeting. The use of "finalize" is jarring, however. It is a favorite word of bureaucrats, so if you would rather not be seen as one, avoid it. You have several good alternatives from which to choose: completed, concluded, made final. As a courtesy and point of information, the writer includes the name of the day along with the date—a nice touch. The personal reference at the end enhances the message.

SEEKING INFORMATION

When you seek information you are asking someone for something, and your letter should be worded accordingly. It should tell why the information is needed and what will be done with it. It should also recognize that the reader is being asked to take some action on your behalf that might not be of immediate benefit to the reader. Reasons for acting should be given, and, if possible, offers of assistance or reimbursement made.

Flawed

LETTERHEAD

Date

Future Publishing Co.
1000 East 51st St.
New York, NY 10000

Dear Sir:

We are developing a Training Course on the subject of Asbestos-Chemical and Toxic Waste Removal, and we are interested in receiving any material that would help us put together the most informative curriculum possible.

If you have any information, publications, or articles on this subject, would you please inform us of the costs involved in sending the information or material to us.

We will be looking forward to hearing from you. Thank you for your service to us.

CRITIQUE: Although this letter will get the job done, it could use some improvement. Apparently, no effort was made to identify a suitable recipient at the company. The impersonal quickly becomes a slight when the salutation "Dear Sir:" dismisses women as recipients. Better to have written "Dear Sir or Madam," "Dear Madam or Sir," or a salutation that is not gender specific, "To Whom It May Concern," "Dear Colleague." Any of these are better than "Dear Sir." The second paragraph does not clearly state what is wanted; it actually asks only for costs. "Yes, it will cost you X dollars" is a literal response to the question. A more effective wording would be: "What information on this subject do you have, and what would it cost to send the information or material to us?" The last sentence, intended to convey goodwill and thanks, misses the mark. "Your service to us" sounds a little presumptuous. "Thank you for any service that you can give us" is better. Even just "Thank you" is acceptable. Finally, the letter suffers from unnecessary capitalization and the failure to use a question mark at the end of an interrogatory sentence.

An effective way to ask for information covering several points is to use a numbered list—one point to a list. Usually, it is enough to state *what* you need. You do not need to give the *why* behind it. That is, you must state your needs explicitly, as in the first paragraph of the sample below—secretarial service, at home, monthly volume. But you need not say, for example in regard to item 3, "I would like to print a small advertisement on each letter if possible." Your short, specific question about the ability to print an advertisement is all that is needed.

Will you please answer the following questions regarding the purchase of your postage meter machine? I operate a secretarial service business in my home. I have a monthly volume of 200 letters.

1. Would I be better off buying or renting your machine?

2. How much does one cost?

3. Does your machine print an advertisement?

4. Does it seal envelopes?

A simple "thank you" at the end will close this letter off nicely. No need to request a "prompt reply" or an answer "as soon as possible." Give your reader credit for assuming you will appreciate a prompt reply.

The letter below, involving as it does state laws, regulatory agencies, and big businesses, could have become an obfuscating exercise in jargon or bureaucratic bafflegab. Instead, it is clearly written, well organized, and to the point, beginning with a statement of the "why" and moving without wasted time or effort to the "what."

Dear Vendor/Manufacturer:

The new Florida "Right to Know Law" that requires employers to provide hazard information on toxic substances is now in effect. The adopted form is the Material Safety Data Sheet.

In compliance with that law, we are requesting that you supply us with a Material Safety Data Sheet (MSDS) for each toxic substance that you supply to our organization.

In addition to supplying the MSDS for toxic substances currently in use, we ask that you provide us with updated MSDS on these substances as new information becomes available. We request that MSDS forms be provided at the time of shipment on any additional substances we may purchase from you in the future.

Your cooperation is appreciated.

SELLING: PLEASANT PERSUASION

Creating the selling letter is an art in itself. People make careers and substantial salaries writing what is called "direct mail." The professional selling letter strives for maximum impact. It must grab the reader's attention immediately, identify a need, and forcefully show how buying the product or service will meet that need.

Unless you plan to make a career in direct mail, you will rarely have the need to write this type of letter. But since all writing must stimulate the reader's attention, and much writing is to persuade the reader to do something, looking at a few direct mail selling letters is worthwhile. (See letters under "Providing Information.")

Flawed

Dear Mr. & Mrs. Martin:

I think you will be excited about the new Recreation Center that was just opened last week at Eden Lake. This exceptional center houses a modern library, game room (billiards, table tennis, card-playing facilities, shuffleboard, and so on), and a little theater in which film classics, as well as our own theatrical productions, are shown. Under construction in the same area are a large swimming pool and a solarium.

This new Recreation Center is just another reason why we believe you will find Eden Lake an ideal retirement community. Although you could not take advantage of our earlier invitation to visit us, the invitation still stands. Why not let us make another reservation for you at the Laurel Mountain Sheraton? Just mail the enclosed card.

CRITIQUE: A soft sell letter, perhaps too soft, although more acceptable than a shrill approach. The weak "I think" beginning and the use of the wobbly "and so on" at the end of the list of activities blunt the letter's impact. Avoid such phrases.

Flawed

NEAL M. BURGESS: YOU MAY BE THE WINNER OF $777.00 A MONTH...FOR LIFE!

Dear Neal M. Burgess:

Now—you a valued credit card account holder, can join one of the most valuable auto plans in the country—you can also give yourself a chance to win a fabulous prize.

Even if you're not the Grand Prize winner, you could still win one of 7777 other valuable prizes including cars, video recorders, and more! The enclosed brochure gives you all the details.

Before announcing our Credit Advantage Road Service ("CARS" for short), we evaluated every major auto club to determine which one could provide the caliber of service you'd expect as an account holder. After long and careful research, we contracted with the Corporate Moguls Auto Club to bring you a plan that we believe offers more for your money than any other auto club in America.

It isn't necessary that you enroll in the Plan to be eligible to win, CARS is one Auto Plan that makes good sense to join. This Plan is quite economical and it provides benefits for you and your spouse on a 24-hour basis.

CARS allows you complete freedom of choice for emergency road and tow service—and reimburses you for up to $60 per call. You can call any garage, service stations, repair shop, towing or wrecker service that you wish and CARS will reimburse you. CARS reimburses you up to $60 per call for the delivery charges of emergency gasoline anywhere you need it, even in your driveway.... CARS will reimburse you for the servicing of snowbound vehicles.... CARS will reimburse you for the servicing of cars disabled in parking lots, muddy fields, beaches, parks, etc. Any car you own, borrow, or rent! (See brochure for details.)

(Three additional paragraphs give more details of the benefits of joining.)

So, please enroll now, while you're thinking of it, and CARS will send you a hand Pushbutton Phone as a SPECIAL GIFT.

Remember, if you aren't completely satisfied with CARS, you can cancel within 60 days for a full credit with a "no questions asked" Money Back Guarantee. It'll take but a few moments for you to join one of the finest Auto Plans in the country. You'll enjoy being a member of the Credit Advantage Road Service.

Sincerely,

President

ps: If you don't mail your entry, the prize that you might have won will go to someone else. Don't let that happen. Return the Official Entry Certificate in the envelope provided.

CRITIQUE: A poor letter in many respects. The punctuation of the first sentence is bad; it is bound to annoy any literate reader. In paragraph four, the first sentence is a run-on. The clauses should at least be separated by a semicolon, but better to make them separate sentences, since the thoughts are not that closely connected. Note also that "ps" should be capitalized; the writer here again displays ignorance of the fundamentals and looks bad as a result.

In general the sentences are poorly constructed, poorly thought out, and disorganized, as are the paragraphs. The overall impression is of incoherence. The tone is similarly inconsistent: After a frenzied opening, the letter goes to sleep. The letter fails to identify any specific need of the reader and waits until the second page to list the benefits of joining. The letter does end with a concrete sales pitch, a spur to act now, and a postscript that refers back to the prize. As it stands, the reader might reply solely to try for a prize. If that is all that is wanted, the letter might succeed.

Dear Listener:

We're worried. Last month Deborah Franklin wrote to you about renewing your membership, and she says she hasn't heard from you yet.

So we got together and decided we'd better write you a letter of our own.

You see, when we're on the air, we feel a special relationship with you. Not only because you're our listener...but because you're one of our members too.

Public Radio depends on you...not just for one year, but year after year. A member who renews is almost more important than a new member. That's because your renewal is what helps us grow and improve our programs for you. It's what enables us to meet the challenge of tomorrow as well as those which face us today.

We want to let you know how much we think of you and

how much we value your participation in your public radio station. We want to tell you that you're as much a part of what makes Public Radio work as we are!

You hear from us every day of the year. Now we hope we'll hear from you...by way of your membership renewal.

Thanks from each one of us!

CRITIQUE: This letter was sent over the signatures of the hosts of different programs. It included their pictures, an effective device to personalize the letter and establish contact with the reader. Although this letter is selling memberships, it is actually a request for donations. The approach here is a frank appeal for help. It works because it is clear, simple, and direct.

BUSINESS LETTER OF INTRODUCTION

Often used as a selling tool, the business letter of introduction can pave the way for company salespeople. It can also be used to maintain and extend contacts.

Dear Mr. Giovanni:

This letter introduces Jill Severn, our Northeastern representative for Extraordinaire Typewriters and Office Supplies. Jill will be stopping by your office next week to show you our latest line of electronic typewriters.

The Extraordinaire Mach 17 is a powerful new machine with expanded memory (the most memory of any comparably priced unit), easy-to-read LCD display, enhanced keyboard (two complete keyboard options plus three "super-shift" keys), and word- and character-correction features.

In addition to the Mach 17, Jill will be happy to discuss our full line of accessories and supplies for all our machines, from hole punchers and pencil sharpeners to calculators and word processors. Please feel free to ask about terms of purchase and our new "Preferred Customer" credit option.

CRITIQUE: This writer is frankly using a letter of introduction as a selling tool. The writer may or may not actually know the recipient. If the writer does not know the recipient, it really is not a letter of introduction, but a sales gambit. If the writer personally knows the recipient—probably as a client—the letter is legitimate and an effective way to use existing goodwill to introduce a new sales rep. See Chapter 9 for other types of letters of introduction.

MAKING A RESERVATION

These are frequently written letters. They must contain the essential information about when you will arrive and how long you will stay. You can add any specific requests and, if required, how you will pay: cash, check, or credit card.

> Jack Vance
> General Manager
> Studio of Light
> 2222 West West St.
> Hartford, CT 06118
> May 30, 1989

Reservations Manager
Grand Hotel
Fifth Ave.
New York, NY 10000

Dear Reservations Manager:

Please reserve a room for me for Friday, June 9. I will arrive at 8:30 p.m., so please hold the room for me. I will leave Monday, June 12, before noon.

I prefer a first-floor room with a shower, double bed, and color television.

Please confirm this reservation and inform me if you will be able to accommodate my specific requests.

> Sincerely,
>
> Jack Vance

Will you please reserve a single room with shower for me for Saturday and Sunday, June 17–18? Because of a late flight, I expect to check in around midnight. Please confirm this reservation before May 15.

CRITIQUE:　These two simple letters are direct and courteous. They give the essential information—dates when the room is wanted, what particular service is desired, and estimated time of arrival. That last item is important because hotels do not hold reservations after early evening unless paid in advance or notified of a possible late arrival.

CONFIRMING A RESERVATION

Dear Mr. McCarthy:

This confirms your reservation for two at the Four Winds Motel from Wednesday, September 23, to Tuesday, September 29, at a rate of $80 per night. The rate includes color TV with cable, private bath, and complimentary coffee and croissants on weekends.

Rooms are held until 6 p.m. unless special arrangements are made. If you expect to arrive later, please inform us as soon as possible so that we will be sure to keep your room for you.

Thank you for your reservation. We look forward to having you as our guest.

CRITIQUE:　A confirmation letter could be a brief form letter of one or two sentences, simply verifying the pertinent information. The sample above went beyond that, however, and took the opportunity to detail available services.

ASKING

Asking people to do something requires finesse. You must make clear why they are particularly appropriate for doing what you ask. Your tone should be complimentary, but not effusive. You must say exactly what is needed and indicate what support you can provide. For example, asking someone to give a speech, unless you are offering a large fee, is asking a lot. The person must devote time to preparing as well as to delivering the speech. The following letters have an effectively persuasive tone.

Dear Ms. Johnston:

You have hired students part-time from our office education cooperative training program since its inception. On several occasions you have discussed with me the advantages, for both students and companies, of the program.

Many employers are unfamiliar with our school's cooperative training program and have asked me to schedule a program to inform them about it. Given your experience and interest, I believe you would be an ideal person to speak to them.

Would you be interested in making a 40-minute presentation to the Chamber of Commerce, December 20, at the Ambassador Motel? The luncheon begins at 11:30 a.m. Your talk would be at 12:30 p.m.

Let me know if you can make it. I will be happy to pick you up shortly after 11 a.m. on that day to provide transportation.

Mrs. John Castanaro
President
State Association of Administrative Services
4321 High Street
Hometown, State 00022

Dear Mrs. Castanaro:

This is to invite you to be the guest speaker at our State Office Education Association Leadership Conference Awards Banquet, April 10, at 8:30 p.m., in the State Suite of the Mall Hotel in St. Paul.

The banquet concludes a three-day conference at which 2000 students from high school office-education courses throughout the state compete in contests to measure achievements. Awards are presented to first-, second-, and third-place winners by the state supervisor of Business and Office Occupations.

Your address of approximately 30 minutes should reflect the importance of competition in our society.

As speaker, you will receive an honorarium and travel expenses. We hope very much that you will be able to accept this invitation. If possible, please confirm by March 10.

Sincerely,

Frank Martin, Association President

In the sample below, the writer is a professor at a university writing to ask a friend and colleague to lecture to a class on his recent experiences. The writer makes the invitation easier to accept by giving the reader more than one date from which to choose.

Dear Bob:

Welcome back to the States! I trust your trip was successful in all ways.

It just so happens that I'm covering fieldwork with my ethnomusicology students this semester, and I'd love for them to hear someone talk about the pleasures and perils of collecting music in the field. Having just returned from a music-gathering trip to Africa, you seemed the ideal candidate.

I have three dates open right now: September 23, 30, and October 7 (all Wednesdays) at 10:05 a.m. The class meets in room 312 of the Social Sciences building on campus and runs approximately 50 minutes. The focus is pretty much up to you; I'm sure anything you have to say on the subject will be appropriate. Slides and/or other visuals will of course be an extra bonus.

If you can make it, try to let me know by next Thursday (September 10). I'm looking forward to hearing about your trip!

AGREEING

It is a good practice to repeat the details to make sure you have the correct information. You should also ask questions to clarify any points you are not sure of. If you are agreeing to give a speech, include some biographical material as a courtesy as well as to ensure that you are introduced correctly. It also helps to say what points you will cover in your talk if that is not clear.

Dear Mr. Martin:

Thank you for inviting me to speak to the high school students attending the State Office Education Association Leadership Conference at the Mall Hotel in St. Paul, April 10. I am delighted to accept.

How long before the 8:30 p.m. starting time should I arrive? Could you send me a program so that I can brief myself on the order of events?

Enclosed is my photograph and biographical sketch, which can be used for publicity and for any introductory remarks you may wish to make.

Best wishes for a successful conference. I look forward to being a part of it.

Dear Jill:

I'm still recovering from culture shock, but yes, I'd love to talk to your students about field recording. I had a wildly successful trip. Ghana and Mali were especially rewarding, both in terms of the music I found there and the people I met.

I'd like to focus on the need for good communications skills when making recordings of traditional music. Very often we are asking to take home someone's wedding, initiation, or even funeral on our tapes. It's absolutely vital that we understand what we are doing and that the local people appreciate why we are doing it. Otherwise misunderstandings and hard feelings can result—which can affect future collectors as well.

The third date you mentioned—October 7—is best for me, Jill. I'll bring slides of my trip as you asked. If you have a tape deck I'll bring some music as well.

Looking forward to seeing you.

DECLINING

Saying no in a letter is one of the more difficult writing tasks. Keep it simple—indicate appreciation for having been asked, give a legitimate reason, and close.

Dear Ms. Alther:

Thank you very much for your kind invitation to speak before the Western Cartographers Association next month.

Unfortunately, prior commitments make it impossible for me to accept your very flattering offer. My work takes me abroad quite frequently, and I will be in Upper Volta the week your association meets.

Please accept my sincere apologies, and I hope you will think of me again if the WCA needs a guest speaker at some future date.

The letter below is barely acceptable. The person invited to speak is very prominent and very busy and must resort to having an assistant decline the many invitations to speak that she cannot accept. This response has the tone of a form letter. Unless you are so busy and in such a position that you need no longer care about how others react to you, avoid this approach. Better to decline in your own name—even if your assistant drafts the letter.

Flawed

Dear Alicia:

Erica Budge conveys her regrets at being unable to address your student group. As I'm sure you are aware, Ms. Budge receives many invitations to speak. Much as she would like to, she is unable to accept them all, regardless of their merit. She has asked me to convey her best wishes to you and your group, and to thank you for thinking of her as a possible guest.

Sincerely,

OFFERING CREDIT: GOOD NEWS

When you have good news to give, give it right away:

> Congratulations, you have been approved for a BANK-FIRST CREDIT CARD!

Usually when credit is approved or a credit card issued, limits, payment dates, and interest rates must also be given. Present such restrictions or qualifications clearly in a positive way. Do not blunt the impact of your cheerful message with a negative tone.

Dear Mr. Althus:

Congratulations! We have opened a revolving credit account in your name as you requested in your letter of June 1.

Your regular 30-day account allows you to charge up to $500. Your statement will be sent to you on the 15th of each month. By paying within 30 days, you avoid a finance charge of 17.5 percent.

You will enjoy the convenience of buying now and paying later, the ease of telephone ordering, and the special savings for regular charge customers.

Use your new charge account privileges at Great-Line's Super Saver Sale coming up in 2 weeks!

Dear Mrs. O'Keefe:

It is my pleasure to tell you that your application for credit has been approved. Thank you for joining more than half a million other customers in doing business with us on a regular basis.

You may begin to charge against your $2500 line of credit immediately.

It is now our job to make sure that you continue to feel welcome and confident in us. It is my job especially to see that all of our staff here at Wonneger's "roll out the red carpet" each time you come into our store.

Dear Ms. Schultz:

Thank you for your application for credit with Randolph Boot and Shoe. You have been accepted and your $50,000 line of credit will become active the first of the month.

Please note that if you pay within 10 days of receiving the monthly statement, you will receive a 2 percent discount. Otherwise, payment is due within 30 days of receipt of the statement.

Credit is a special privilege granted only to qualified businesses. It is my pleasure to extend this service to you and your firm. Welcome!

REFUSING CREDIT: BAD NEWS

Give bad news without giving offense. Search for a positive way to state the negative. While you do not want to begin with a stark rejection, neither do you want to raise false hopes that will result in bitterness when dashed. Include valid, acceptable reasons for the rejection. Do not, however, attempt to soften the blow by hinting at the end of your letter that an application might be granted in the future, unless this really is likely. If there is genuine hope for a positive response later, say so, and say what conditions will warrant the change. (For more on refusing credit, see Chapter 2.)

Dear Mr. Snow:

Thank you for applying for credit at Durfee's Department Store. It is always a compliment to have cash customers request credit.

Although we would like to approve your application, we cannot do so at this time. A routine check of your credit standing revealed you have unpaid balances of several months' standing at other businesses.

We will be happy to consider a new application in 6 months after you settle those accounts. Until then, we hope that you will continue as a cash customer to take advantage of the many sales and savings that we offer.

Dear Mr. Evans:

Thank you for sending us your financial statement and your application for a line of credit. You will be happy to know that your credit references spoke highly of you as a beginning businessman.

Your new business is located in one of Waterford's busiest shopping centers and has all the conditions necessary to prosper. However, our records show that two other restaurants have not been successful in your location. Until we have an opportunity to see what your experience is in Mall Square, we must ask you to deal with us on a cash basis.

To help your restaurant succeed, we are offering you a 5 percent cash discount rather than our customary 2 percent. May we suggest that you order small quantities of supplies frequently, keeping enough stock on hand to cover your weekly business, so you can keep your cash outlay low.

We would welcome the opportunity to review your application again after a year's operation. May it be a prosperous year for you.

SEEKING PAYMENT: UNPLEASANT PERSUASION

Asking someone to do something she or he does not want to do is one of the more difficult writing tasks. Many companies, of course, resort to the form letter for collection efforts. Nothing wrong with that, especially if the form letter is an effective one.

Keep in mind when writing demanding letters that the written word packs a lot of power. A shouted spoken word can startle and frighten, but it fades and is forgotten. The written word lasts; it is unchangeable, and it is solid, tangible evidence of what is communicated. It can be seen by many people.

For these reasons, when writing to persuade a reluctant individual to pay or to take an undesirable action, you should let the facts speak for themselves. Avoid harsh words and threats. State the facts along with clear instructions as to what action to take. If the receiver's failure to act will result in increased efforts on your part (getting a lawyer, hiring a collection agent, higher penalty costs, going to court) say so in a cool, straightforward way without threatening words. The actions described are threat enough.

To achieve compliance, you often must mount a campaign that involves several letters, beginning with gentle reminders and moving in one or two stages to insistent demand for immediate action and a warning of the consequences of not acting. In the early stages of a writing campaign to collect or force some action, allow for the possibility that the person has already taken the action you desire, and, for example, a check is in the mail, as the first sample below does. This first sample is a simple form letter. The body of the text would be on file. The name, address, amount owed, and extent of time owed would be inserted as required.

Dear _____:

This is to remind you that your account is now_____ months overdue.

If you have already mailed us your check, please disregard this notice. If not, use the enclosed envelope to send us your check for $__.__ immediately.

Dear Ms. Allwether:

This is our second letter reminding you that you still owe Labrador Hospital $333.48.

When you made application for admission and asked for hospital care, we gave it immediately, explaining that payment was due in 30 days.

Your remittance of $333.48 must be returned today. A stamped, addressed envelope is enclosed for your convenience.

Dear Mr. Jones:

On August 5 you were notified that Eastern Auto Renewal had placed your account with us for collection. However, we have still received no response from you.

We must receive the full payment of $350 by October 15, or we shall be forced to take further steps to collect this amount.

Please make your check payable to Pequot Finance and send it today.

OFFERING A JOB: GOOD NEWS

Offering a job, like offering credit, is a "good news" letter, so get right to the point. Make it clear what is offered and why.

Dear Mr. Trump:

Would you be interested in writing a book on the subject of organic fillers and resins for publication by Northland Press? I read your article on this subject in the December 1986 edition of *Issues in Plastic* and believe that this topic could be expanded into a full-length book.

Northland is a publisher of technical and reference books with a sizable list of books for the plastics industry. One of our best-selling books is the *Manual of Reinforcements and Fillers for Plastics,* edited by Harry Katz. This book, however, has only limited coverage of organic fillers. I would be interested in considering a book on this topic alone that would be a minimum of 250 printed pages.

If this idea interests you, I would be glad to discuss it with you further. For your information, I have enclosed a catalog of our chemistry books and guidelines for preparing a manuscript proposal.

I look forward to hearing from you.

Dear Bill:

Congratulations! You have been chosen for the position of Program Manager at WXYZ FM Radio.

After an extensive process of reviewing applications and résumés, interviewing applicants, and discussion, we of the Program Committee have agreed that you have the most desirable combination of skills, experience, and attitudes that we have been able to find.

As you know, WXYZ is a small, listener-supported station serving a wide range of needs and tastes. Your job as program director will be to balance music and information programming so as to reflect the diversity of our audience and the philosophy of the station. A complete job description is enclosed.

The salary and benefits will be as discussed at our last meeting. A contract is being drawn up now and will be sent to you as soon as we hear from you. The position becomes vacant as of the end of next month; I assume there will be no difficulty for you in starting on the first.

Once again, Bill, congratulations! We look forward to having you as a member of the XYZ community.

The sample below is not a definite job offer, but a form letter sent to qualified potential candidates offering them the opportunity to apply for a position. This is a tactic that search committees for large academic or business organizations sometimes use to generate a list of candidates from which to make a final selection. It is impersonal and cool. The approach can be effective, particularly if the organization is prestigious and the potential position coveted. For a small organization with an average job opening, this is not an effective strategy.

Dear Professor of Philosophy:

Applications are now being accepted at Omega State College for an assistant professorship in philosophy. Interested parties are requested to submit a résumé and salary requirements to the dean of faculty at the above address.

The successful candidate will be expected to teach two general, introductory classes in Western Philosophy, one intermediate course in the philosophy of the Enlightenment, and one upper-level course in a subject of his or her choosing.

Please submit a sample course description, including reading list, for one of the courses described above (not including the upper-level course) with your résumé.

Sincerely,

REJECTING A JOB APPLICANT: BAD NEWS

Without being rude or blunt, get to the point quickly. Do not raise false hopes with a flattering beginning. And do not raise false hopes about possible future employment if in fact the likelihood is non-existent or very small. Find something complimentary to say about the individual being rejected, but do not overdo it or you will seem insincere. If there is a particular reason that can explain the rejection in a way that salves the ego, state it. End by expressing good wishes for future success.

Avoid the passive voice. It does not soften the rejection to present it passively: "Your application has been rejected." A person being rejected would prefer it done by a human being and not an unnamed power.

Dear Ms. Johnson:

Thank you for taking the time to apply for the position of office manager that we recently advertised.

I am sorry we will not be able to offer you the post. You were one of many qualified applicants we interviewed, making it a difficult choice for us. The successful applicant had the most experience in our particular field.

I wish you luck in your job search. I am confident that you will find the type of job you seek, as your qualifications and personality are excellent.

Dear Albert:

After a careful review of your résumé, I regret that we are not able to offer you the post of chemicals supervisor at this time.

Our company seeks individuals with outstanding academic backgrounds, which you possess, as well as several years of experience in the field.

We feel that you would benefit by more hands-on experience before you begin to work in a position of such responsibility and difficulty. We hope that you will keep us in mind as you gain experience, because we are always in the market for energetic men and women of your potential.

Thank you for thinking of United Chemical. We wish you success in your career.

Sincerely,

Dear Ms. Waters:

We regret to inform you that the position for which you applied, word processor/data clerk, has been filled.

We are sorry that we cannot offer you employment at this time. This should in no way be considered a reflection on your abilities.

Best of luck in your job search.

RESIGNING

Do not burn your bridges with a resignation letter—particularly if you are leaving in anger. Convey your negative message in a positive way. State your reasons for resigning as compelling. If you sincerely regret leaving and have something favorable to say of your experience with the organization, say it. If you do not, do not. Especially do not take this occasion to air grievances. Do not underestimate the written word's power. Harsh words that are spoken fade from memory. Written words are more permanent and remain unchanged even if conditions change to make you rue them—such as a desire to return.

Ms. Alice Santos,
President
Santos Landscape
PO Box 12B
Franklin, CT 06664

Dear Alice:

As you know, I plan to establish my own company, Green Tree & Landscape, and therefore submit my resignation as vice president of Santos Landscape, effective in 1 month.

Please make necessary arrangements to amend the corporate records. Feel free to contact me if you require any further action on my part.

It has been a pleasure to be associated with you and Santos Landscape.

Sincerely,

Sam Goldberg

Dear Bill:

Reluctantly, I offer my resignation, effective June 1. As you know, there are personal considerations that I have ignored too long and that now urgently require my attention.

My experience with Smith & Jones has been a very positive one. I have benefited from the association with my colleagues here in ways that I cannot fully enumerate. My admiration for the philosophy of the firm and the opportunities afforded its employees is tremendous. I leave with deep regret.

I sincerely hope that you will continue to enjoy the greatest success.

Dear Mr. Salzburg:

I regret that I must resign my position at Elwin, Elwin, & Co., effective October 15. An opportunity has been offered me by another company that will allow me more time with my family, and I feel I should accept.

I leave Elwin, Elwin, & Co. with the highest regard for you and the other members of the firm.

Dear Mrs. Carrothers:

Please accept my resignation as secretary/receptionist at the Research Department effective June 10.

Since I plan to move to Seattle, Washington, on July 1, I will need a few weeks to get things ready and packed. If you wish, I will be happy to train my replacement.

Thank you for the opportunity to work with your Research Department. I learned a great deal, both about my own job and the work of the Department in general, which I am sure will be valuable to me in seeking future employment.

Respectfully yours,

SUMMING UP

This chapter gives you many samples of typical business letters written to achieve different goals. Whatever your immediate goal, keep in mind that the underlying goal of any business letter is to persuade or sell. After you have written your business letter and are satisfied that it fulfills your immediate goal— giving or seeking information, refusing credit, asking for money, and so on—read it again, while asking yourself, "Does it sell?" You'll know what you should do if the honest answer is no. Yes, rewrite.

7

Effective Memos

Memos (short for memorandums, or memoranda if you prefer the Latin plural) are the most commonly used form of written communication in business. Some people think they are used altogether too commonly and dislike what they perceive as a glut of unnecessary memos.

Memos are informal *interoffice* communications that note or record something worth sharing or remembering. You would not write a memo to someone outside your company—you would write a letter.

Occasionally an organization selling through direct mail will use a memo format in its mailings seeking customers:

TO: Jane Doe, 11 Plank St., Gary, CT 00660

FROM: XYZ INSURANCE CO

MESSAGE: URGENT—PLEASE READ IMMEDIATELY

After this memo format opening, the text pitches a hard sell for insurance. The intention is to convey a businesslike impression and a need for immediate action. It is gimmicky. Restrict memos to interoffice communications.

THE CYA SYNDROME

In many businesses, especially large ones, a major, if unstated, purpose for writing and sending a memo is to protect oneself. Memos written for this purpose, while purporting to be serving one of the legitimate goals of communication, are known as CYA (for cover your you-know-what) memos.

MEMOS ARE NECESSARY

In some companies, the flood of memos has become so great that top executives have written memos urging employees to stop writing memos. But that is a little bit like passing a law saying it is illegal to break the law—a rather futile exercise.

Although overworked and at times misused, memos remain an integral and necessary part of the daily business routine. Memos do perform useful work as a medium of written communication as the samples, listed by category below, demonstrate.

A memo's value is that it leaves a record. A quick telephone call or face-to-face oral exchange doesn't. And even if that need for a record suggests an urge to protect yourself, good written records promote efficient operations. Hence the memo endures, despite its detractors and despite the fact that a lot of memos probably never need be written.

STANDARD HEADINGS

Many companies have forms preprinted with the standard memo headings to save typing time. The headings usually include "To," "From," "Date," and "Subject." Exactly how the headings appear on preprinted forms varies slightly from company to company. The illustrations on the page opposite show three common arrangements. Whatever the arrangement of the elements, however, the "To:" always comes first.

INTEROFFICE MEMORANDUM

To: From:

Company: Company:

Dept: Dept:

Floor / ext: Floor / ext:

Subject: Date:

INTEROFFICE MEMORANDUM

TO:

FROM:

DATE:

SUBJECT:

TO: FROM:

SUBJECT: DATE:

Sometimes memos have lines for titles and divisions or departments of sender and receiver, floor numbers, and telephone numbers and extensions. The rule is to keep it simple. Do not bother with titles unless absolute policy is to use them all the time. Just using your name and the name of the addressee is best. If you want to pull rank, then, of course, use your title.

The *subject* line is particularly useful, since it immediately identifies the purpose of the memo. It also relieves the sender of the need to repeat the information in the body of the memo.

30-SECOND MEMOS

Memos should be action-oriented, direct, and brief: three or four paragraphs. A good letter will impart its message in one minute or less. A good memo should make its point in 30 seconds of the reader's time. Occasionally, a memo must be longer, even longer than one page, but, as a rule, when you have something to say that takes up more than one page, write a report.

Memos are less formal than letters. They are more direct than reports. They should not be chatty. Follow the old newspaper formula in writing memos: Who, what, where, why, and when—and get all these "Ws" in the first two paragraphs. The who is usually you, the sender, and that is made clear by the memo format and your signature. The when, which refers to when you want it to happen, is particularly important if your memo is seeking information or asking for some action to be taken.

MEMO ETIQUETTE

One of the thorniest questions about memos, particularly in large corporations, concerns "who to copy," which is to say, to whom to send copies. Do not confuse who is receiving copies with the addressee. You can have multiple addressees. When sending a memo scheduling a meeting, you will have multiple addressees. (See below for ways to address such memos.)

Knowing the addressee is the easy part. Knowing to whom to

send a copy is not. The general rule of thumb is "need to know." A copy is a courtesy to inform others who might be affected. Usually, you would send a copy of a memo to your immediate boss if your memo affects the department.

You would rarely, if ever, send a copy of the memo to the boss of the addressee. This is a form of pressure or psychological blackmail that most people resent. Consider your feelings if someone sends you a memo asking for information or action and at the same time sends a copy to your boss. You would feel there was an attempt to intimidate you, and you would probably resent it.

As a matter of information and courtesy, you should send copies to anyone you mention in the memos, but use the "cc's" on your memos with care.

A questionable tactic is to send a bcc or blind copy. That is, you do not note on the original or let the receiver know that a copy of the memo is being sent to someone else. This is particularly underhanded if the blind copy goes to the receiver's boss. About the only legitimate use of the bcc is to send a copy of a memo to your own boss, just to keep her or him informed about some action you are taking—if the receiver has no interest in who else gets a copy.

CATEGORICAL SAMPLES

In the remainder of this chapter, you will find several samples, both good and bad, of memos arranged generally according to their purpose: to share information, seek information, praise, and warn. Interspersed with the samples are comments and tips on the art of writing an effective memo.

Although the categories reflect a practical arrangement of memos by function, any one memo could serve more than one function. You might need to write a memo that both shares and seeks information. Generally, though, try to focus your memos so that they clearly convey their message to the reader.

Sharing Information

The briefest memo for sharing information consists of the receiver's name (addressed as you would normally address the person), the initials "FYI" (for your information), your initials, and the date written on a copy of the information you want to share:

Dave,

FYI

Bud 9/24/90

When sharing information, avoid the urge to share too much, which is a common problem among memo writers. In the following example of a poor memo, the writer attempts to share information, pass on instructions, and issue a warning of sorts, and fails to do any of them effectively.

Flawed

TO: Project Sponsors

FROM: William Radley

DATE: 7/8/89

SUBJECT:

I will not be in the office Friday, July 11 through July 25. It is important that we continue to present projects for signing. I will read and approve all projects submitted to me prior to my leaving. All other projects that are not read should be discussed with me. These projects, not read, but discussed, can be processed for signing.

Our signings through June, 44 in total, are very low; need I say more. Last year we signed 120 projects, and we need to sign at least that many in 1989.

I know that each person and their assistants are aware of the challenge before us. With budgeting and reports behind us we should begin to get some projects presented and signed. We need some long working hours and while I am out I expect everyone to continue as normal. Any issues that require my signature should be processed as normal and Ethel and Carlo will see that Jack Cornwall signs the documents.

CRITIQUE: Beginning with the failure to list a topic at the subject line, this memo declares the writer's lack of thought and organization. It begins simply as an informational memo, telling the sponsors that the writer will be out of the office during a certain period. Then, still sensibly, it instructs them on procedures to follow during the absence.

Then the memo becomes a warning about poor performance and an exhortation to encourage better performance. As a memo to encourage greater effort, consider the effect of the sentence: "We need some long working hours and while I am out I expect everyone to continue as normal." Asking people to work harder in the same sentence in which you say you will not even be in the office will not usually generate the response you wish. But this sentence is so unclear, the reader cannot be sure the writer really is asking everyone to work longer because it ends, "I expect everyone to continue as normal." A few sentences previously, however, the implication was that normal was not acceptable because "Our signings through June...are very low."

Because of poor wording, the reader cannot really be certain whether he or she is to continue submitting projects during the boss's absence. In the first paragraph, the boss seems to suggest that *only* those projects he has seen should be presented. Yet in the final paragraph, he says to continue sending *anything* requiring his signature.

The sloppy grammar is a further clue to the writer's problems. He has a run-on sentence, fails to use a question mark after a question, and fails to have noun and pronoun agree in number. By themselves, none of these errors is fatal. Together with the disorganized presentation of material, they destroy whatever effectiveness the memo might have had. About all this memo accomplishes is to generate disrespect for the writer.

The first improvement is to make at least two memos out of this one. A serious production problem is worth a memo by itself and should not be treated as an afterthought tacked on to a memo informing others the writer will be out of the office. Coupling a notice of the boss's absence with an exhortation to the troops to work harder borders on the ludicrous.

The use of "I" and "we" is awkward. (There is no you element at all.) The excessive "I's" jar: "I will...I will...I saw...I know...I am...I expect...." Their use is especially irritating since the "I's" all appear in negative statements or in statements about being away. The "we's" appear in sentences talking about the work that has to be done: "we continue...we signed...we should...we need some long working hours...."

The statement "I will read and approve all projects submitted to me..." makes the reader wonder why to submit projects if the writer is going to approve them all anyway.

Improved Memo (No.1)

TO: Project Sponsors

FROM: William Radley

DATE: 7/8/89

SUBJECT: Absence from Office

I will be away from the office Friday, July 11, through Friday, July 25. [If for business reasons, say so.] It is important that during my absence you continue to present projects for signing. I will review all projects submitted to me prior to my departure. Please submit as many as possible before I leave.

Projects and other documents that require my signature should be processed as normal while I am gone. Ethel and Carlo will see that Jack Cornwall signs the documents.

Improved Memo (No.2)

TO: Project Sponsors

FROM: William Radley

DATE: 7/8/89

SUBJECT: Need to Sign New Projects

Everyone should be making extra efforts to sign up new projects. In June the total of new signings was only 44, an unacceptable level. Last year sponsors signed 120 projects, and we must at least equal that number this year.

I know that each of you is aware of the challenge before us. With budgeting and reports behind us, we should be able to concentrate on getting projects presented and signed. I will work closely with each of you to help increase the number of signings.

Among the important memos you will write are those summarizing actions taken at a meeting. If you are at a high level in a large organization, you will probably have a secretary take notes and draft the memo that contains the minutes of the meeting. If you do not have a secretary and are responsible for the meeting, you must do all the work yourself. In any case, the memo should be approved by you before it is sent out.

Memos conveying the minutes of meetings at which tasks were assigned and deadlines set should be specific and direct. The following sample summarizes a meeting of a book development team of editors, designers, and production personnel.

TO: Development Team   FROM: B. Sawyer

SUBJECT: 5/27/91 Meeting   DATE: 5/28/91

The following actions and dates were agreed to at this meeting:

- Bound book date is 3/5/92.

- Anne and Robert will give production dates for receiving art this week.

- Jim will provide cover costs by 7/10/91.

- Photo research will provide costs this week.

- Design department will give production art specs by 6/12/91.

Please inform me if there are any errors or omissions.

TIP: Ending the memo with a request for the readers to inform the writer of possible errors or omissions is more than a courtesy. This request encourages a closer reading and some extra thought and allows the writer to share the burden of recalling what was decided.

Seeking Information

Memos seeking information should be brief and to the point. One or two sentences usually are sufficient. Be sure, of course, to identify exactly what you need and to state explicitly a time by when you need to receive it.

TO: Ruth McConnell   FROM: William Sampson

SUBJECT: Invoice Reporting   DATE: April 26, 1990

Ruth, please send me copies of invoices the day you receive them.

Thank you.

TO: Department Heads*   FROM: R. Miller

SUBJECT: Performance Review   DATE: April 7, 1991

Lois Black of the Professional Development Department will be interviewing me concerning the Performance Appraisal Program.

I would like each of you to send me your comments on this program no later than Wednesday, April 21.

Thank you.

*L. Caine
P. Lydon
M. Millard
R. Montaigne

TIP: In the memo above, the title for all addressees is the same. Just the title with an asterisk is put on the To line, and the names of the managers are listed in alphabetical order at the bottom. This is a standard way of addressing a memo going to several different people. If the titles are different for each person, you can use the word "Addressees" on the To line, followed by an asterisk to indicate the names listed at the bottom.

To: William Sole   From: M. Roger

Subject: Cost Estimates Project Q

As we discussed, please send me the backup documentation (invoices where available, otherwise estimates) for the final costs for this project.

Warnings

Memos are often used by managers to give written warnings to subordinates or to provide a written record of an oral warning. Clarity is particularly important in such memos. The warning memo must be written so there can be no mistaking *what* is at issue, *why* it is a problem, *what* can be done about it, and *when* action should take place. The "what" should include a recommended course of action, and the "when" a specific deadline for taking the action.

The sample memo below was written in response to the discovery that employees were deciding without prior managerial approval when to work overtime. The result was that payroll budgets for the departments were being exceeded as workers put in for unauthorized extra pay. The general manager had to warn department managers about the practice and its negative results and had to suggest a solution.

TO: Department Managers

FROM: General Manager

DATE: 7/1/89

SUBJECT: Working Overtime

In recent weeks, several departments have been exceeding their overtime budgets. It appears employees are deciding on their own when to work overtime.

People in your department should notify you when they expect to work overtime so that you can determine whether it is necessary and whether your budget can afford it. The people in your department should never work overtime without your prior approval.

Extra costs for overtime are charged against your cost center. You are responsible for maintaining your overall budget.

It is your responsibility to keep your employees informed regarding overtime policy.

Writing warning memos is one of the more unpleasant tasks a manager faces. The memos should state the problem in a straightforward manner without being rude or excessively critical. The memo should always suggest a course of action, give a target date for remedial action to be taken, and be positive. One way to convey a positive tone is by giving the impression that improvement is possible and anticipated. In the sample below, the manager was documenting an oral warning about excessive tardiness.

TO: Sara Burke   FROM: Hugh Ouellete

SUBJECT: Tardiness   DATE: 4/4/91

Sara, I sincerely regret the need to give you an oral warning concerning the tardiness of yourself and your department. We had discussed this problem before and for a time there was some improvement. Lately, however, the situation has again deteriorated.

The record shows that for the past 7 months of this year, you have arrived at work late (9a or later) 62 times. Martha Monez, a member of your department, has arrived late on 91 days during this period. This record of tardiness far exceeds what company policy regards as excessive.

We all have a commitment to be here during company working hours. Tardiness creates conditions that are bad for morale and for the efficient operation of the company.

I ask for an immediate and sustained improvement in punctuality. I am confident you will correct this problem for yourself and your department.

I shall review the situation with you in 3 months (7/4/91).

Setting Up Meetings

Memos setting up meetings should be brief. They should include the date (the day of the week as well as the month), the time, and the place of the meeting. Also, they should include an agenda or list of topics to be discussed. If a particular action is expected to result from the meeting, that should also be indicated.

> TO: Julius Navarr
>
> FROM: Leona Traveller
>
> Please plan to attend a meeting Tuesday, 9/25/90, at 2:30p in conference room 2002 to discuss marketing plans for the coming holiday season.
>
> We will set the seasonal marketing budget.
>
> If you are unable to attend, please send a representative in your place.

Sometimes you must send a memo to several different people to set different meeting dates for each. The following example shows the simplest way to do so. The manager was setting up performance appraisal meetings with several different people reporting to her.

> TO: J. Dewer, M. Jones,   FROM: May Rodin
>   S. French, R. O'Neill
>
> SUBJECT: Performance Appraisal   DATE: 12/3/90
>
> Please plan to meet with me in my office for your 4Q performance appraisal at the date and time shown.
>
> J. Dewer—1/7/91 Mon 10a
>
> M. Jones—1/7/91 Mon 2p
>
> S. French—1/9/91 Wed 10a
>
> R. O'Neill—1/10/91 Thurs 1p

TIP: In memos use abbreviations and the shortest form whenever possible: 4Q for fourth quarter; 1/7/91 instead of January 1, 1991; Mon instead of Monday; the letters "a" or "p" immediately after the time to signify morning or afternoon. Be sure the abbreviations or short forms are clear.

Sometimes you might not have a specific date for a meeting but need to meet with people before a particular deadline. Let them set the date within a given period, subject to your confirmation. This approach can reduce going back and forth to find a mutually open date. It also is courteous to let others, particularly subordinates, select the date. It is a good approach to take when having to call a meeting on a sensitive subject, such as performance reviews.

In the sample below, the sender reminds department managers they must complete the performance reviews of those under them by a specific date and invites them to set a date for the review of their own performance.

TO: Department Managers*

FROM: General Manager [Name only is sufficient]

DATE: 8/5/91

SUBJECT: Midyear Performance Appraisal

We are required to complete the 6-month performance appraisal review of all employees and send the written reports to personnel by the end of this month. Please complete the reviews of those reporting to you so as to have the signed reports on my desk for my action no later than 8/23/91.

For your performance appraisal, please call my secretary, Juanita, to schedule a meeting sometime during the weeks of 8/12/91 or 8/19/91. Please have the date set no later than 8/8/91.

*J. Dole
 M. Kneeland
 W. Orlandez

Giving Instructions

Giving instructions is very difficult to do in writing. Be specific and include all necessary instructions. The common fault of most memos giving instructions is that they attempt to be *too specific* and they give *too much* instruction. In the example below, the general manager of a division wants to stop production on the Curley Project.

Flawed

TO: Production Supv   FROM: General Manager

SUBJECT: Curley Project   DATE: March 25, 1991

Because of unexpected costs and a declining market, it has been necessary to review current works in progress for the purpose of identifying those that are unlikely to be successful, so that they may be terminated at this time and the production money reallocated to speed up the development of those that are likely to be successful.

The Curley Project was one of those reviewed. Please take appropriate action immediately in accordance with this review. It is important that the potentially successful projects not be delayed.

This memo says more than it needs while not stating the necessary instructions. The production supervisor might conclude that the Curley Project was one of those to be pushed ahead.

Improved

TO: Production Supv   FROM: General Manager

SUBJECT: Curley Project   DATE: March 25, 1991

Unexpected costs and a declining market have made it necessary to review current works in progress to identify those unlikely to succeed. Those so identified are to be terminated and the production money reallocated to more promising projects. The Curley Project was one of those identified as unlikely to succeed.

Stop all work immediately on the Curley Project.

Sometimes when writing instructions, we trip over the simple things, perhaps because we assume that if something seems simple or clear to us, it is clear to the reader. A good rule to follow in any writing, but particularly in giving instructions, is *never assume* any knowledge on your reader's part. In turn, you must avoid the other mistake of trying to tell too much, as mentioned earlier. Striking the balance of telling enough without telling too much is the writer's constant goal—especially the writer of memos that give instructions.

In the next sample, the writer was careless in construction, probably because she assumed the reader would know what she meant. The memo was just a note to give instructions to a person replacing the writer who was going on a month's vacation. The writer owned a small flower shop.

Flawed

TO: Janice   DATE: 6/27/89

Thanks for filling in for me.

It is important that you water the plants and feed them fertilizer. Be sure you do not do this more often than every other week because too much food will hurt the plants.

See you next month.

Unfortunately, when the owner returned many of the plants had died from lack of water. She assumed the replacement would know you water plants more often than you feed them fertilizer and thus wrote a sloppy note that actually told the replacement not to water the plants often. A better memo would have been:

TO: Janice   DATE: 6/27/89

Thanks for filling in for me.

It is important that you water the plants every other day. Feed them fertilizer only every other week, because too much food will hurt the plants.

See you next month.

Compliments

Do not use memos for compliments except in casual situations. If a person deserves a compliment, the person deserves the formality of a regular letter that can be proudly shown and even framed. A memo has the appearance of having been dashed off in an offhand manner and thus is not suited for the sincere compliment. Occasionally, you might want to give someone a pat on the back or a quick morale booster, and a short "well done" memo can serve that purpose.

If you wish to compliment someone for having written a good article or report, you could simply make a copy of the first page and write:

"Great report!" or "Fantastic article, I loved it!"

and sign and date it.

A short memo to compliment an individual on doing a job particularly well or winning the company bowling trophy that year could consist of the traditional headings and just,

"Well done! We are proud of you." Or "Thanks for beating that deadline. We appreciate it."

If you are complimenting someone on having received a promotion, winning a prestigious award, earning an academic degree, write a letter.

A common use of the complimentary memo is for one department head to thank another for special attention or effort in the line of work. In the sample below, the production manager thanks the marketing director for having invited the production manager and supervisors to attend the annual sales meeting.

The purpose of the invitation was twofold: to reward and recognize the production department with a rare trip, and to give the production personnel a chance to get input directly from the field sales force. Although it was primarily business, a complimentary or thank-you memo was in order.

TO: R. Gore, Mktg Dir.   FROM: S. Levine, Prd. Mgr

SUBJECT: Annual Sales Mtg   DATE: 8/12/91

Bob, for myself and the supervisors, I want to say "thanks" to you and the marketing division for the warm hospitality extended us last week at the annual sales meeting in Great Gorge.

The organization and execution of the meeting were impressive—as was the morale. It was informative for those of us in Production, and we appreciated the opportunity to meet with the field staff. (We also enjoyed the kind words we heard.)

Please share this memo and our appreciation with all those involved in making our attendance so pleasant and worthwhile.

A memo sent to a work team for having done a particularly good job helps build goodwill and boosts morale.

TO: Textbook Production Team   FROM: N. Olds

SUBJECT: Well Done   DATE: 7/13/91

Everyone who has seen it has been extremely impressed by the textbook you produced. Our director of marketing said, "The textbook is beautiful. More books that look like this and we can't be stopped. Please extend my sincerest thanks to your staff for this outstanding job."

Outstanding is right.

Job Promotions

Writing memos recommending someone for promotion is a pleasant task. Do not approach it offhandedly. Another person's future depends on your effectiveness with the written word.

If you are writing to your superior or other higher-ups to recommend that someone below you be promoted, you have to persuade them by your objective praise of the individual. Keep your praise objective and not effusive. State explicitly the reasons for your recommendation of this person in terms of performance and how the promotion will help the company.

State exactly the nature of the promotion and what the exact raise will be, the yearly cost to the company, and whether the money is budgeted if you have responsibility for budgeting.

TO: N. Williams   FROM: M. Juarez

SUBJECT: Promotion for C. Lowell   DATE: 9/12/90

I recommend that C. Lowell be promoted to Supervisor,

Level 1. She is currently Supervisor, Level 2, a position she has held for 3 years.

In her present position, C. Lowell was responsible for overseeing the completion of Project Math 1 and Math 2. I am very pleased not only with the technical skills she has acquired, but also with her attitude: She volunteers for work, and she is taking courses evenings to increase her knowledge.

The promotion will increase her salary from $18,000 to $20,000 a year. The budget for the remainder of this year includes money to cover the cost of this promotion, which is approximately $500.

Thank you for your action on this.

TIP: The writer of this memo includes all the necessary information, such as what position the person has now, how long she held it, *specific* reasons for recommending the promotion, what the cost will be, and whether there is money in the budget.

Requesting Action

When making a written request, be as specific as possible. You won't be standing before the individual to make immediate clarifications. If you are unclear about what action you want, the best that will happen is that there will be a delay until you have made a clarification. The worst is that you will get some action you did not want.

Do not clutter your message with explanations. Your reasons are usually clear from the nature of the request. If a reason is called for, give it succinctly. Concentrate on the request and write to the point.

TO: Personnel (Name) FROM: Dept. Head (Name)

SUBJECT: Secretary DATE: 8/9/90
Replacement

Betty White, my current secretary, has been promoted to the position of assistant bookkeeper effective 9/1/90.

Would you please immediately begin the necessary paperwork to obtain a replacement for her?

Thank you.

TO: Dolores Sanchez   FROM: John Sawyer

SUBJECT: Telephone Directory   DATE: 9/30/91

This is to order a telephone directory with 10 buttons for the workstation outside Sam Frank's office (rm 2805 on the 28th floor).

The following extensions are to be on the directory: 6722, 2179, 4310, 2288, 3713, 6633, and 3218. All buttons are to light up except ext. 6722 and 2179.

The remaining buttons are for hold, intercom, and signal.

Could this be installed by 12/1/91?

Thank you for your help.

The next-to-last sentence is in the form of a question, which sets a deadline in an oblique way that may be less likely to ruffle feathers than a direct command: "Please install this by 12/1/91."

Tip: Many people end memos with phrases like "Thank you" or "If there are any questions, please contact me." If overused these phrases become meaningless time wasters. Many people feel, however, that memos look abrupt, unfinished, or even rude without them. The purpose of using a memo, of course, is to avoid some of the conventions of a formal letter, but these phrases have become a form of complimentary close on a memo. A trend to drop the complimentary close on business letters exists, so be sparing in using closes in memos.

The following memo requests action. It is a relatively minor matter—the writer must determine which product managers will be at which conventions the remainder of the current year and during next year. In some ways, it is a good memo. It is brief and to the point. The topic is clearly stated on the subject line, and the necessary schedules are attached. No words or time are wasted repeating any of this information in the body of the memo. The memo explicitly states *what* is wanted and *when* it is wanted.

But the overall professionalism of the memo and the writer's credibility are marred by the misspelling of two key words. Since both words are repeated in this short memo, the misspellings become painfully obvious.

Flawed

TO: See Distribution* [names listed alphabetically at bottom]

FROM: S. Barrows

DATE: 9/29/90

SUBJECT: 1990 End-of-Year Exhibits
     1991 Exhibit Schedules

Attached are two separate schedules:

1. End-of-Year's Schedule
2. Next Year's Schedule

Please send both back to me by the end of next week with your committments. A committment means setup, booth time, and breakdown.

If you know at this point that your schedule allows for partial attendence (or no attendence) at a show because of prior committments, please let me know.

Thank you.

The key words "commitment" and "attendance" are misspelled. The memo's message does come across despite these errors, but, unfortunately for the writer, another message also comes across all too clearly. Spelling does matter. Check yours.

SUMMING UP

To paraphrase Shakespeare, brevity is the soul of the memo. If your memos go on for pages, something's wrong. Either you need to cut a lot of unnecessary material, or you need to break the memo up into smaller memos that cover single topics. Don't write the Great American Memo—just write the one that gets the job done.

Avoid the memos-for-their-own-sake trap. If you have a job that needs to get done, a message that needs to be distributed to a number of people quickly, or some other pressing reason, then write a memo. If a phone call or 2-minute conversation will do the job, do it that way. Save paper, time, and effort.

8

Reports

Any writing—letters, memos, minutes, notes, a diary entry, news release—is report writing in that facts are written down to be remembered or communicated. All forms require the same writing skills. When we talk of a report, however, we have a specific kind of written document in mind. A report:

- Is prepared in response to a perceived need
- Requires research
- Contains a collection of facts organized and analyzed to arrive at conclusions
- Is usually long (3 or more pages)

In academic writing, the conclusions of a report (thesis, term paper) are valued for their own sake. In business writing, report conclusions are used as the basis for making decisions and taking action.

Often reports, especially in business, are written as the result of committee action; that is, a problem was identified and a committee appointed to investigate it, gather the facts, and make recommendations. Although the report is the result of group action and the final report must be approved by the group, the actual writing of it will be assigned to one person. In this situation, the quality of the research depends on the group effort, and the quality of the written end product will depend on one or two individuals with others making suggestions or editing.

AN OUTLINE—THE FIRST STEP

For any long writing project, begin with an outline. Consider the major points you think must be covered and the order in which they are to be presented. As noted, a report organizes and presents facts to arrive at certain conclusions. Write a description of each point, in one to three words.

Some points are more important than others. The outline should reflect this. Any outline has different levels of entries or headings. In publishing, these levels are often referred to as a 1 head, 2 head, 3 head, and so on. They can also be called level 1, level 2, level 3, and so on. A 3 head introduces a subsection after a 2 head, which in turn introduces a subsection after a 1 head. You will rarely have more than three levels; often you will have only one level.

The rule of outlining is that you must always have more than one occurrence of a level. You would not have a report that had just one 1 head, or any subsection with just one level 2 or level 3 heading within it. The system's logic is that if there are not really two sufficiently important ideas to warrant headings, the text should not be broken up. If a relatively short report seems to require only one 1 head, it probably does not require any head other than the report title.

Making an outline forces you to think about your report and how you want to organize it. The outline will change as you conduct research and prepare the report. The outline should serve as a guide, not an inflexible rule. Without the outline as a guide, writing a long report can be an impossible chore.

RESEARCH IS VITAL

To write a good report, you must have good research skills as well as good writing skills. Research is particularly important. If your research is poor, even good writing skills will not enable you to prepare a good report.

There are three ways to conduct research; that is, to gather the facts you need to write your report. Which you use will depend on the reason for writing the report. These three ways are: (1) *interviewing,* (2) *observing,* and (3) *reading.*

For business reports, interviewing and observing are probably used most. For academic reports, reading usually dominates. All three will be used to some extent in any kind of report writing. An excellent book on research skills is Alden Todd's *Finding Facts Fast,* (2d ed., Ten Speed Press, Berkeley, Calif., 1979).

GOOD NOTES = GOOD REPORTS

Whatever method you use as you conduct your research, you will take notes of the facts you want to include in your report. If you do not take adequate notes, you will not be able to write an adequate report. To a large degree, the quality of your final report will depend on the quality of your original notes.

As with so many creative efforts, good note taking requires mastering the art of doing enough without doing too much. Too few or sketchy notes will result in errors, lost time, and incomplete facts. Too many notes will result in errors, lost time, and poorly understood or revealed facts. If you try to note down every detail in an interview or when observing, you will probably miss the significance of what you are hearing or seeing.

To ensure that you take adequate notes, have a clear idea of exactly what your report is about before you begin. Identify the problem to be researched, form an idea of what outcome is desired, and, as noted above, develop an outline. Knowing the desired outcome does not mean knowing the conclusions or recommendations. You must know the scope of the problem to be addressed or of the knowledge desired.

Many people use 3 by 5 cards for taking notes, devoting each card to one point. Later you can rearrange the cards to reflect the order in which the points or facts will appear in your report. A disadvantage of the cards is that they are small and can be easily misplaced. Also, they fill up fast. Using regular paper on a clipboard might work better. You can put as few notes as you want on each sheet and still have room for adding much more material if necessary.

TIP: Whether you use cards or paper, write on only one side. Notes written on the reverse side of a card or sheet of paper are easily overlooked.

A notebook of whatever size is okay, but you will have to tear out the pages if you want to reorder your facts.

If you have access to a computer with a word processor while taking notes, use that. With a computer you can rearrange notes easily. Also, when you write your report, you can copy the notes directly into the report without retyping them. Computers, however, have obvious limitations for note taking. They are bulky (even the laptops), they require power, and, fast though they are, you can get a pen and paper working faster.

BASIC ELEMENTS

You will find reports in all shapes, sizes, and formats. Reduced to their essentials, all reports contain three basic elements, which for simplicity's sake can be called: (1) the *introduction*, (2) the *body*, and (3) the *conclusion*. A fourth element, the *executive summary*, has become popular, almost standard, in large corporations and even small companies that like to think of themselves as on the cutting edge. Contrary to what you might expect (and to normal usage), the executive summary comes not at the end of the report but at the very beginning, even before the introduction.

The information contained in the executive summary is often included instead in a transmittal letter or memo that accompanies the report. The phrase "executive summary" has a ring to it that echoes nicely in many a bureaucrat's ear, however, so it is frequently used. When an executive summary is used, the transmittal letter or memo need be only a sentence or two stating the report's name, its basic purpose, and that it is attached.

The Introduction

In the introduction you give the *reason* the report was prepared, *who* prepared it, and *how* it was prepared. The reason is a factual statement of the problem or the situation that prompted the report—in other words, the need the report is intended to meet.

As with each section, you would precede the introduction with a heading, which could be "introduction" or perhaps "facts" or "need." The heading would be put on a line by itself, in all capital letters or underlined for emphasis.

Introduction

Many employees voiced concern about congestion at the normal 8:30 a.m. and 4:30 p.m. starting and quitting hours. The congestion has resulted in increased tardiness and inconvenience. Employees find it necessary to leave home earlier in the morning, and they arrive home later in the evening.

Staggering the starting and quitting hours to reduce the number of people moving in or out at one time was suggested as a possible solution. The general manager named a committee made up of one representative from each department with the personnel director as chair to study the feasibility of staggering hours. The study had two goals:

1. To determine if staggering hours would help reduce congestion

2. To determine whether enough employees would be willing to start and stop work at different hours to make the program work

The committee obtained employee views through a company-wide survey form, which also allowed each individual to indicate preferred working hours in four different combinations.

In addition to the survey, several employees in each division were interviewed. The committee also interviewed local police officials, managers of public transportation lines, and representatives of other companies in the area to get their views of the commuting situation as well as their reaction to the proposed plan.

This sample introduction explains the need—to reduce traffic congestion; tells what was studied—staggered hours; tells who did the study—department representatives with the personnel director; and tells how it was done—with a survey and interviews.

The Body

The body is the main part of your text. It is where you put your findings and discussions. You would set it off with another subhead, such as "Findings," which is a general heading that can be used in any report. The body will include a section at the end discussing or summarizing the findings.

In a long report, break up the solid blocks of text with subheads at natural breaks in the subject matter. For the report on staggered hours, additional subheads could be: "Survey Results," "Employee Interviews," "Traffic Official Interviews," "Area Business Interviews," and "Summary" or "Analysis of Findings."

Your subheads should reflect the divisions of your report as indicated in your outline. The major sections of your report are, as noted, introduction, body, and conclusion. Each of these sections would carry a level 1 head. Long sections, such as the body, can be broken up with subheads, first level 2 and then, if these subsections require further division, level 3 heads.

The report on the study of staggered hours to relieve traffic congestion could have these headings:

Introduction

Findings

   Survey results

   Employee interviews

   Traffic official interviews

   Public transportation official interviews

Area business interviews

Analysis of findings

Conclusion and/or Recommendations

If the report is particularly long, you could break up the body (Findings) further with the use of level 3 heads:

Introduction

Findings

Survey results

Interviews

Employees

Traffic officials

Public transportation officials

Area businesses

Analysis of findings

Conclusion and/or Recommendations

TIP: There are always at least two occurrences of each level of headings. The interview section is set off by a level 2 head and is further divided by four level 3 heads.

Within the body of the text, you have a subsection summarizing or analyzing the findings. For the sample used, this subsection of the body of the report could look like this:

Analysis of Findings

A majority of employees favored staggered hours, and the survey indicated sufficient interest in earlier or later hours to ensure a workable spread.

Traffic officials welcomed the idea of staggered hours and felt they would definitely help relieve traffic congestion.

Public transportation officials said they would adjust bus and train schedules as necessary.

Neighborhood businesses indicated an interest in the idea and a willingness to cooperate to help it work. (For example, the local coffee shop said it would serve breakfast early and late enough so that all could eat there regardless of time starting.)

The reduction of traffic congestion will reduce tardiness and increase efficiency and morale because workers will spend less time getting to and from work.

This section leads directly to the last major section.

The Conclusion

As indicated in the section above, the heading setting off this section can be "Conclusion and Recommendations" or just "Conclusions" or "Recommendations." At this point, the report writer states the recommendations as briefly and clearly as possible. A standard procedure is to present multiple conclusions as a numbered list. For the sample we've used, this final section might look like this:

Recommendations

1. A schedule of staggered hours with four starting times (7:30, 8:00, 8:30, and 9:00), with quitting hours adjusted accordingly, be tried for 6 months

2. Supervisors in each department be responsible for assigning hours with employee choice based on seniority given priority insofar as possible, so long as one quarter of staff is on duty during staggered working hours

3. Review by committee in 6 months to determine effect on traffic congestion, tardiness, efficiency, and morale

The Executive Summary

If used, the executive summary becomes the very first page of your report. It summarizes on one page what the report is all about and what it recommends. An ideal summary might consist of three paragraphs (the idea is to be brief), each devoted to one of the three parts of the report: introduction (need), body (findings), conclusion (recommendations). The executive summary allows the busy individual to see the highlights at a glance. If the busy individual is interested, she or he can subsequently read the details.

Some advocates of the executive summary say it is a time saver. Others say it will catch the interest of a busy individual who might otherwise not find time to read your report. On examination, these become rather feeble reasons for having the executive summary. Anyone could acquire the gist of the report in seconds by glancing at the pertinent sections, guided by your headings, so little time is saved by the reader. Creating the executive summary takes more time than it saves, which results in a net loss of time to the company.

However, these executive summaries are popular in many areas. If in doubt, go with the flow—write one.

TIP: Using the copy function of a word processing computer, you can create an executive summary rather quickly by simply copying the pertinent parts to the summary.

An executive summary of the staggered hours report might look like the following:

Executive Summary

Traffic congestion has created problems for the company and workers. The feasibility of staggering starting and quitting hours to relieve the situation was studied by the committee.

Employees, traffic control officials, public transportation officials, and other area businesses were contacted through surveys and interviews. Staggered hours were found to be feasible and a possible relief for congestion.

The committee has recommended a 6-month trial with starting hours staggered to 7:30, 8:00, 8:30, and 9:00 a.m.

OPTIONAL ELEMENTS

If you wish to dress up your report, you can include additional elements. If you are working in a large organization, if your report is going to many people, or if it is a particularly large report, you should consider including some of the following options. They can impart an air of professionalism to your report.

Title Page

Even a small report can use a title page (some might feel a small report requires a title page to lend it weight). A title page should include the title of the report, the name of the committee or of the committee members, and the date. It can be on letterhead paper.

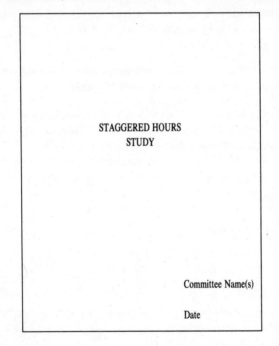

Table of Contents

If your report runs to many pages (15 or more), a table of contents is a useful courtesy. By listing all the elements and the pages on which they start, you achieve much of the effect of an executive summary.

The table of contents simply lists your headings with the number of the page on which they start. Many word processing programs can generate these tables automatically. A sample table of contents follows:

TABLE OF CONTENTS

Introduction 1

Findings 2

Survey Results 3

Interviews.. 6

Employees 8

Traffic Officials 11

Public Transportation Officials......................13

Area Businesses..15

Analysis of Findings 18

Conclusion/Recommendations 20

Bibliography

For long reports based mostly on reading, you should include a bibliography at the end. A bibliography lists the books, magazines, articles, and other reports that you have read for the report. It is a courtesy and helpful to the reader, and it enables the reader to evaluate your sources and supplies the necessary information for finding and reading those sources.

Each entry in the bibliography should include the author's name, title of article, name of book or periodical, the volume and issue number, name of the publisher, place of publication, and date of publication, in that order. Arrange the list in alphabetical order by authors' last names:

Davis, Nathaniel B., *Traffic Congestion Relief,* 3d ed., Tidal Press, New London, Conn., 1988.

Holmes, Susan M., *Staggered Hours Save,* Business Press, New York, 1987.

SUMMING UP

Do not be intimidated by having to write a report simply because it is longer and requires more research than your normal writing. The same principles apply for reports as for any other writing. If you can organize and write a good letter or good memo, you will have no trouble writing a good report. A report will probably contain more than one point. Fine. Take it one point at a time and use the knowledge in the various chapters to write to each point.

SECTION FOUR

EFFECTIVE WRITING AT HOME

Section Four explores the various types of writing at home, including writing to friends, for the sheer pleasure of it, for action (complaints, information), for a job (résumés and "fishing letters"). Whether you want to improve your holiday thank-you notes, spice up your letters home, or organize your job-hunting letters, what follows will interest you.

9

Writing for Pleasure

Writing letters was once a source of pleasure, an invaluable tool for communicating vital news, and a way to bridge distances that were otherwise insurmountable. Even when friends lived no farther away than across town, the exchange of letters was a dynamic aspect of the relationship. The letters of famous and not-so-famous people are part of our literary heritage and are invaluable sources of information about our past.

Today, of course, the preeminent place of the written word in long-distance communications has been challenged. Paradoxically, in this age of automated labor-saving devices, people feel they don't have the time to write letters. The telephone has to a large extent replaced the letter as the most common way for friends to keep in touch. Nevertheless, the letter has three qualities that recommend it even in this age of electronics: permanence, perspective, and tangibility.

A letter can be filed, looked at, used like a journal or a photo album to recall times past. If you go back and look at a letter you received—or sent—years ago, you will probably find things you had long since forgotten: facts, feelings, incidents. This has a practical application in law and business, but it has value in our personal lives as well. It is a record of important parts of our lives and relationships.

Perspective in a letter means you can stop and think about what you are going to say before you say it. In personal writing, you can explore a feeling, an adventure you had, even a beautiful scene out the window, in ways that a conversation will not permit. Letters achieve a certain depth because you can take as much time as you need to say what you want, you can bring in related ideas, and you can make your sentences fit your thoughts.

A letter's tangibility, in addition to making it a permanent record, means that it has a kind of presence that a conversation on the phone does not. If you get a phone call from a faraway friend, it is wonderful to hear her or his voice—nothing can substitute for that, short of the friend's actual presence. But, once the call is over, that's it. There's nothing to go back to, to keep the image of the person fresh. A letter, although it does not have the immediacy of a phone call, remains a visible record of the person. If the day after you receive the letter you find yourself thinking about the friend, you can go get the letter out again, look at it, refresh your memory and your mental picture of your friend.

WRITING TO FRIENDS

When writing personal letters, remember that it should be *fun*. There is no point in writing a letter like this out of a sense of obligation. You do it because you care about your friend and you enjoy talking to him or her. Try to think of it as a conversation in which you get to do all the talking!

Write what you feel. Don't worry too much about style, grammar, or even punctuation or spelling, so long as the letter is intelligible. Your friends will forgive minor errors. They're more interested in what you have to say than how you say it. Once you've written it, you can make any corrections you feel are necessary before you send it.

Try to write about things of mutual interest. This does not mean you have to write "newsy" letters. They can be about anything— how you feel about your new job, about a movie you saw last week, about your latest get-rich-quick scheme. Write whatever interests you. Your interest is the surest guarantee of your reader's interest.

Some people have a mental block about writing, the way others do about math. For these people, writing will never be anything but a chore, and the telephone is a blessing. If you are one of these people, you probably don't write many letters anyway—mostly quick birthday cards and the like. But if putting words to paper is not sheer drudgery for you, you may find that writing letters for the pleasure of it is a richly rewarding way to explore a relationship, new or old.

This chapter has samples of personal letters, but remember there is no typical personal letter. On the contrary, the samples should give you a taste of the incredible diversity possible when writing among friends.

In the first sample, two friends are collaborating cross-country on a homemade magazine they hope to produce. Because the work on the magazine is between friends, it is combined with a personal letter. You can do business in a personal letter.

Dave—

Again I write from a park—having just seen the finale of "The Other Opera"—a big arts-council-funded piece with orchestra and chorus leaping from a barge as the sun sinks behind the Olympic Mountains. Big-time art extravaganza. After swimming ashore they performed on the large rock sculpture for the last two pieces. The crowd was whooping and hollering. Now it thins and darkness sets in.

I am glad to hear of your mood, the place you are, the space you're in. I've tried to call you off and on for the past month to see what was going on—and wondering/hoping you might be persuaded to move out here. It would certainly make working on the newsletter easier.

So what do we do? I agree with all the suggestions in your previous letter. It occurs to me that you'll end up doing most of the work if indeed you put it into the word processor. I think it would be easiest if we coedit it and Fred & I send you the articles we can contribute—then you can send me the proofs for layout. I want to do it, but I'm uncertain if I have the time to do it all *and* do a very good job. I think if we collaborate it could be great.

I'll be calling you about this. Eventually, I'll be buying a computer—probably this winter—but it'll still take me a while to learn how to use it. The one you're using looks good—what kind is it?

I was hoping that I'd be seeing you—you'll have to come visit at least...I'm building a "guest suite."

Take care,

The next sample is a keeping-in-touch note, but that doesn't mean it is brusque. On the contrary, it has a very special warmth that is no doubt appreciated by the recipient.

Dear Bill,

Hi! I just wanted to get in touch since I felt sorry that we missed each other over your birthday weekend. Did you end up coming to Boston or not? At any rate, I hope you had a nice birthday. I'd like to hear about your job, life, etc. The work sounds interesting—does it still feel strange not to be in Virginia? What has the transition been like?

It seems strange that summer is just about over, eh? I just came back from my last camping trip of the season, on the Cape. It's been amazing to get out of the city so much and by the ocean, lakes, woods....Work is still very demanding and I tend to get too anxious about it—but it also feels like I'm starting to get a handle on it....Anyway, enjoy the New England autumn as it comes in.

Love,

Another keeping-in-touch note, but this time with some other work to do as well:

Dear Joan,

It was so good to hear your voice, and I am very much looking forward to your joining me in NYC for dinner in the event that you will not be able to hang around this Friday (so keep in touch!!).

I am still touched by your sweet gift. Thank you again!

Take good care of yourself!

Best always,

The following example is actually a postcard dashed off in a hurry. Keep in mind, however, that not all personal letters are necessarily short. Some can go on for pages and pages, about anything at all— books, relationships, the weather, cars, football, music, computers, philosophy, nature, science, politics—whatever you feel like discussing with your friends.

10 June 1987. Kyoto.

Dear Alfred—Wow! How long has it been? Is it two letters I owe you? (Plus interest!) I never wrote with my plan? No? What am I thinking of? Well, right now, the U.S.

World Conference at GWC on L.I. 19–30 June. Please give me a call!

I'm flying out next week. I'd love to see you. Just sent a card to Wally and I hope to see you both in the Big Apple.

Happy New Year!

Don

COMMUNAL LETTERS

Communal letters are sent by one person or family to a group of friends or relatives. They are personal letters, usually mostly news of recent events, but they do not contain private or sensitive information. They are usually, but not always, sent during the winter holidays as extended greeting cards.

Reactions to communal letters are mixed. Some people find them annoying, even insulting in that the recipients are receiving copies not original letters. Others find them useful and enjoyable, both to send and to receive.

TIP: Send communal letters only to family and close friends. Imagine getting a letter describing what's happened in the lives of four people over the past year whose names you don't recognize—someone you met at a convention or a wedding, for example. Don't burden casual acquaintances with personal news.

If your family is far-flung and has trouble keeping in touch, communal letters help keep everyone connected. You can bring people up to date on where grandparents, brothers-in-law, nieces and cousins are, what they are doing, who has been married, who has had children, who has moved away. More than just bringing the news, they help create a sense of belonging and community that is difficult to maintain when one brother lives in Tucson, a sister in Seattle, the parents in Colorado, and so on.

If you are going to write a communal letter to several people at once, keep it short—one or two pages, keep it pleasant, and keep it among friends.

Three friends are working on a homemade magazine together; each one lives in a different city. One of them wants to share his reactions and ideas with the other two, so he writes one letter and sends it to both of them. It is a practical application for group letters that can be used by small clubs and the like.

Dear Lisa & Bruce,

I have received the first issue of the newsletter & wanted to give you my comments. I'd be willing to do proofreading on the next one. I have the experience & the eye for it. If it seems feasible to do over these long distances, I'm up for it.

In fact, I'm up for doing the typesetting, though in this day & age you can't really call it that. I'll have access to a computer and a laser printer which supports all kinds of nifty stuff like italics, boldface, small caps, strikethrough, underline and double underline, superscript and subscript. This is not to mention, of course, the spelling check & general ease of keyboarding, revision, & such that a good WP provides.

Which means that the newsletter can look fancy if we want it to. And if we decide it's feasible to send MS across country for this purpose. Let me know what you think.

One thing this printer can't do yet—or that we don't know how to make it do—is graphics. However, graphics would be nice, don't you think?

Lisa: I liked your articles. I was impressed with the amount of fact/info you were able to integrate with the overall theoretical viewpoint.

Get back to me,

CONGRATULATIONS

The letters in the following categories—congratulations, thank you, invitations, accepting or declining, introduction, reference, and condolences—are all somewhat formal types of letters. There are more-or-less accepted conventions for each of them that make writing them easier in some ways but harder in others. They are easy because the format is already set; you just fill in the blanks. They are hard because, when writing formulaically, it is difficult to sound sincere and personal.

Congratulations letters depend on the occasion for the congratulations. The usual form, however, is to open with a simple sentence to the effect of, "Congratulations for [whatever the occasion is]," or "We were happy to hear...." This can be followed by an expression of your wishes for the reader's future success, by an elaboration on why you feel the honor is particularly deserved, or perhaps an appropriate offer or suggestion (a celebratory dinner, an offer to share the news with friends). The close can be a simple reiteration of the opening idea.

To a Friend on a Promotion

Dear Jerry,

I read in the Journal last night that you've been named senior partner at Olsen, Olsen & Ross. It's a fine old firm, and you are fortunate, but *they* are the real winners.

It will be a pleasure to inform any of your old pals who may have missed the news in the paper. Good luck in the new position!

Congratulations again,

On the Birth of a Baby

Dear Alice,

We were delighted to hear the news of Max's birth. Congratulations to the whole family!

I'm looking forward to meeting Max, and having a chance to visit with you and Carl again. I'll call when I know the next time I'll be in town.

Looking forward to seeing you. Until then, all my best.

On an Engagement

Dear Bonnie,

George & I are thrilled to hear the news of your engagement! Clyde is one of our oldest and dearest friends, and we have long felt that you and he would make a wonderful couple.

Our warmest best wishes to you and congratulations to Clyde on getting such a wonderful person. We are so happy for both of you and are eagerly awaiting the day of the wedding.

Traditionally, you offer congratulations to the man, not the woman. The idea is that the man was the pursuer and is to be congratulated for having persuaded the woman to be his wife. She, this rationale goes, had unlimited choice and congratulating her suggests otherwise: that she was lucky to get a man. Send the bride-to-be best wishes for the future. But this tradition is often not followed today.

THANK YOU

The thank-you letter is a simple letter or note that many people dread writing, probably because it often seems difficult to sound sincere.

If you are writing mostly from a sense of obligation, the main thing is to keep it short—don't give yourself an opportunity to sound like you don't mean it. If you *do* mean it, of course, that will probably come through if you choose words that feel natural to you, the kind of words you would use in speaking.

Almost as important as brevity and sincerity, if not more so, is promptness. A thank-you letter that comes 6 months late will not sound sincere, no matter how natural the diction or how genuine the sentiment. Above all, respond immediately if possible, or if not, as soon as you can.

For a Wedding Gift

Traditionally the bride writes the thank-you notes for wedding gifts. Although etiquette allows some leeway for honeymoon and settling down, the sooner written, the better. You can purchase special notepaper for these thank-you letters in any stationery store. Be enthusiastic. Try to say how you will use or have wanted such a gift—but do not force it.

> Dear Ms. Jones,
>
> The tea set is delightful! Ted and I are, as you probably know, avid tea drinkers, so we'll get many hours of use from this beautiful gift.
>
> Our warmest thanks and kind regards to you and your husband. Do let us hear from you again.

For Birthday or Holiday Gifts

> Dear Phil,
>
> How did you know I was a science fiction fan? (Need I ask?) Believe it or not, I'm already half-done with the novel—I sat down with it the minute I opened the package, and couldn't be budged until dinner time! It's a winner, all right.
>
> Regards to Jill and the kids. Hope to see you all next Christmas.

For a Baby Present

Dear Aunt Irene,

Sally looks <u>adorable</u> in her new snowsuit! It's so pretty, and the size is <u>just right</u>. I've enclosed pictures so you can see what a hit your gift has made with the whole family.

Thank you so much. I hope you'll pay us a visit one day soon.

Other Thank-You Notes

Other thank-you notes are also common. For example, if someone has done you a favor—offered hospitality to a friend, put in a good word for you with a prospective employer, put you in touch with someone—you certainly owe them a thank-you note. Here is a letter written to someone whose name the writer was able to use on his résumé during his job hunt. He got the job, and wants to let his reference know that he appreciates the help.

Dear Professor DeRosa,

I think you will be pleased to learn that I have been hired by Kyodai Corporation to work in their Research and Development Department. The company manufactures chemicals, and I've been told that my first assignment will be to research applications in film and paper preservation methods.

Thank you for allowing me to use your name as a reference. I am certain your recommendation carried a lot of weight in Kyodai's decision to hire me. I will do my best to prove that I deserve your confidence.

I hope to see you from time to time to let you know what—and how—I am doing. When you are next in Olympia, please visit me at my office. The company is located at 1100 Evergreen Boulevard.

INVITATIONS

Invitations are probably the most standardized personal letters and therefore the easiest to write. (The only thing that's hard is the fact that there are so many!) Invitations come in two basic styles, formal and informal.

Formal invitations are often printed professionally. They often include a form and envelope for reply. The information is centered on the inside of a card, in several easy-to-read lines:

Mr. and Mrs. Allen Ludlum
request the pleasure of your company
at a dinner to honor
Judge and Mrs. John Gould
Friday, the second of March
at seven o'clock
International Suite
Eden Lake Hotel

RSVP:
134 Euclid Ave.
Glen Spey, NY 12745

Informal invitations take the form of a very brief note that includes the time, place, and nature of the function; directions if necessary; and a phone number or address to which to respond. Be careful not to clutter up this important information with less relevant material.

Dear Ted & Alice,

We're having a little get-together next Friday with some of the gang. We'll have a light dinner and people can stay as late as they like. We've asked everyone to arrive by 6:30; dinner will be at 7:00. If you can't make it, give us a call; otherwise, we'll be expecting you. See you then!

Bob & Carol

Dear Raoul,

It was a pleasure meeting you last week. Since you're new in the area, Norman and I thought you'd like a chance to meet some of the interesting folks in the neighborhood.

We're having an informal party on the 13th and we'd love for you to come. It'll be starting around 7:00, but come whenever you can. I've enclosed directions. Give me a call if you think you'll make it; the number is 555-1397.

ACCEPTING OR DECLINING

Like invitations, responses are fairly straightforward. Again, avoid clutter. If you do have something to say other than "Yes, I'll come" or "Sorry, can't make it," keep that part of the message separate from the rest. That way, your host gets what he or she is most interested in without having to dig through a lot of other material to find it. In responding to formal invitations, of course, you won't say anything, really, except yes or no—more would be inappropriate. Formal invitations often include a form for the response. If no form is enclosed, a brief note in the same manner as the invitation is sufficient:

Dear Mrs. Yamamoto:

Mr. and Mrs. Allen F. Goldstein are delighted to accept your invitation for dinner on the 19th of June at 11 Court St., Gary, CT, at 6:30 p.m.

Sincerely,

A phone call is considered an acceptable way to respond to an invitation. Remember to confirm the time and place.

A quick note (or phone call) will suffice to respond to informal invitations, as long as it contains the necessary information:

Dear Carol,

Thanks so much for your note! Ted and I will be there, of course. The date, just to confirm, is a week from Saturday, at 6:30.

By the way, I saw Fred the other day, and he asked me to give you his best.

Alice

Declining an invitation takes the same form as accepting one. Don't explain in detail why you can't come. Simply respond promptly and

phrase your reply as courteously as possible. Again, in the case of
the formal invitation, the format already exists.

> Mr. and Mrs. Allen F. Goldstein regret that they are unable
> to accept your invitation for dinner on the 19th of June. Prior
> commitments unfortunately make attendance impossible.
>
> Sincerely,

And for informal responses, the degree of casualness depends on
your relationship with the host or hostess.

> Dear Lois,
>
> Thanks a lot for the invitation. I'm afraid I can't make it,
> though, as I've already made plans for the evening.
>
> Thanks again, and I'm sorry I won't be able to attend. I know
> I'll miss a great time.

INTRODUCING

A letter of introduction can be a social or a business letter. Its purpose is to tell someone you know, a friend or business acquaintance,
that the person carrying the letter is known to you and that you can
vouch for him or her. Since it usually includes or implies a request
for hospitality, do not send social letters of introduction to people
you do not know well—only to friends you feel comfortable asking
a favor. To do otherwise is to presume.

Your friend, Alicia Waters, is traveling, and you have some
friends you would like her to meet. You want to write your friends
and tell them briefly about her. Below is the letter of introduction
for her to hand-deliver upon arrival. Before that, however, you
would privately contact the person you are writing to—either by
mail or phone—and let him or her know you will be doing this.

At any rate, Alicia should make a point of contacting your friends
before visiting. Usually this means a telephone call when she has
arrived in town. Upon meeting her hosts in person, Alicia would
then present your letter. A more formal letter of introduction:

Dear Mr. Allen,

Alicia Waters is going to be in Berkeley on June 5, during her national tour to promote her latest book of poetry. Alicia is a great friend of ours and has been for many years. I am giving her this note of introduction to you and Mrs. Allen, in the expectation that you will enjoy meeting her as much as I know she would enjoy meeting you.

Fondest regards,

An informal letter of introduction:

Dear Bob,

I am giving this letter to Alicia Waters, a fine poet and very good friend of ours.

She will be winding up a national tour to promote her new book in Albuquerque the last week in June, and I'd be delighted to have her meet you.

Preceding the above, by mail:

Dear Bob,

I have given a letter of introduction to Alicia Waters, for her to present to you upon her arrival in Albuquerque.

In addition to being a fine poet (her new book is just out), she is a dear friend, a witty, charming person, and a big jazz buff. She even does a little singing herself. I'm sure the two of you would hit it off marvelously. I hope you'll be able to meet her when she's in town.

REFERENCES

Reference letters can be written for a friend, a former employee, a former student, anyone you have worked with as a volunteer—in short, someone you have had the opportunity to observe in a position of some responsibility.

A letter of reference or recommendation *never* says bad things about the person in question. To write such a letter would be in bad taste and could make you look like a petty and spiteful person. If you do have a bad impression of the person, simply refuse to write the letter. If the prospective employer wants your opinion, he or she will call you and you can then present your case, objectively and without malice.

The fact that you are not 100 percent enthusiastic about your recommendation should not prevent you from writing one at all. This is one situation where tone, choice of words, and style can say a great deal. They can make the difference between a letter that says, in essence, "He's ok, I guess," and one that says, "He's fantastic! You'd be nuts not to hire him!" Even if your recommendation is only lukewarm, however, give your ex-employee (or student or whatever) the benefit of the doubt and write *something*. This is a very important time in life, and we all need all the help we can get.

A letter of recommendation tells the reader what you consider the strong points of the person you are writing about. Always begin by saying how long you have known the person and in what capacity. Try to provide as complete an evaluation as possible, in all areas relevant to your relationship. For example, if you feel the person is especially good with people, a good team worker, say so. If the person is very bright, learns quickly and accepts responsibilities easily, mention that. Do not limit yourself to the specific duties performed—but be sure to include them too, or at least the most important ones.

To save the person the embarrassment of having to ask for a letter, consider offering to write one—assuming, of course, that it is something you really want to do.

The following samples include letters of recommendation from employers, teachers and friends, for a variety of perspectives on this very important category of correspondence.

A Lukewarm Employer Recommendation

To whom it may concern:

I was Albert Smith's supervisor for one year when he worked as bank teller for Friendly Banks of Westwich. He performed his duties satisfactorily; he was punctual; he was always neat and accurate. I wish him success in his career. I am sorry we could not provide the level of salary and responsibility Mr. Smith desired.

An Enthusiastic Employer Recommendation

To whom it may concern:

It has been my privilege to supervise Albert Smith for 1 year in his capacity as teller at Friendly Banks of Westwich. During his employ he performed difficult tasks under great pressure with skill and alacrity; every duty he was assigned he undertook with enthusiasm. He demonstrated unusual skill in dealing with the public—unusual even in an environment where we demand the best in human relations skills. His interaction with his co-workers was no less positive. In fact, he was a real boost to morale during his entire tenure here.

Albert is an exceptional employee whose talents and personality will make him a wonderful addition to any firm. I only regret that his personal plans have prevented him from continuing with us at Friendly Banks.

A Teacher's Recommendation for a Favorite Student

To whom it may concern:

Roberta Olsen has been my student in history for the past 2 years at Wilbur Wright High School. During that time she has progressed remarkably in her studies. She has always been a quick and eager learner, and she has taken full advantage of the opportunities available to her.

Roberta is a mature, intelligent young woman, and I would happily recommend her for any endeavor she chooses to undertake. I would be pleased to answer any questions you may have, and may be reached at the above address.

Sincerely,

A Personal Reference

Dear Ms. Althea:

Thank you for the opportunity to give my impressions of Joyce Turnbull. It is indeed a pleasure to recommend her for any post for which you may consider her.

I have known Joyce for over 10 years. She is a close personal friend and has worked with me in a variety of community organizations and volunteer groups. I have always been impressed by her intelligence, her talent for organization, her sense of responsibility in whatever effort she makes.

To give just one example, we worked together to raise funds for a local charity for 6 months. Joyce was elected chair of the committee in charge of fund-raising, and it was largely due to her inspired leadership that the campaign was a success.

I will be happy to answer any questions you may have about Joyce's work and abilities. I may be reached at 444-6655, during business hours.

CONDOLENCES

As noted in Chapter 2, the condolence letter is a very personal letter whose tone, feeling, and sincerity are most important. One sample condolence letter appears in Chapter 2; more are presented in this section.

Express your sympathy in as natural a manner as possible. Avoid being too emotional or effusive, however. In general a restrained tone is preferred. Even between close friends a measure of formality is expected. Think of how you would dress for the funeral: you want to show that you feel grief, but you also want to show respect.

Keep the letter brief. Lengthy discussions, no matter how germane, are an unwelcome intrusion. Confine your message to an expression of sympathy and, if you feel it is appropriate, something about the deceased that you especially admired. If the bereaved is a close friend, an offer of help—"anything I can do at this time"—can be included.

Dear Mrs. Johnston,

Edward and I were deeply sorry to learn of your husband's death. As you know, we were both his students. I don't think either of us had a teacher who was more inspiring, warm, encouraging, or who taught us more.

Our thoughts are with you in this time of grief. Mr. Johnston will be missed by many of us.

With deepest sympathy,

Dear Frieda,

The news of Carlos's death was a terrible shock to all of us. We share your grief, Frieda. Carlos was a dear friend to us all and leaves a gap that can never be filled. His humor, his insight, his loving kindness were rare and wonderful qualities that we loved and learned from.

Of course we are all ready to help you with anything you may need. Don't hesitate to call if you are feeling overwhelmed. It is the least we can do.

With love and sympathy,

Dear Mr. Bowles,

I was very sorry to learn of your wife's death. Although I did not know her personally, I knew her by reputation, and through her work in the community.

Please accept my deepest sympathies at this time.

Sincerely,

SUMMING UP

This chapter covered two basic categories of writing: writing for pleasure and personal writing such as thank-you notes and invitations. Writing for pleasure is the easiest writing there is, and there's really only one rule to follow: if it's no fun, don't do it. If you like to write letters or want to give a friend or relative a boost, then go for it. Otherwise visit, use the phone, use ESP, but don't torture yourself with something that should be a joy for all concerned.

As for the thank-you notes and such—well, there are times when we all have to do them. But again, don't strain. The simplest approach is the best. Say what you have to say and be done with it. Of course you don't want to sound clichéd, insincere, or brusque, but don't try too hard to be original. Most people expect these letters to be rather standardized. Add the personal touch (a fond memory of the deceased, for example, in a condolence letter, or a brief statement of *why* that necktie was just the perfect gift), deliver the message, and sign off.

10

Writing for Action

Writing at home is not all for pleasure or pleasure mixed with business. More often you put words on paper for practical reasons. If you fear writing and thus do not do much writing for pleasure, you have less practice; consequently, when you must write for practical reasons, you have greater difficulty.

Relax. Although letters for action will not have the same chatty tone of letters for pleasure, you can still keep them informal. As with letters for pleasure, when writing practical letters, you want to get your message across clearly and effectively. All the rules of grammar, punctuation, and so on are designed to help you achieve clarity. Use them as helpful tools.

REQUESTING CREDIT

Today you rarely need to write a letter asking for personal credit. You apply for a credit card or a charge account by filling out a form. The same is true if you are seeking a mortgage, a car loan, or money to purchase a big ticket item.

There are still occasions when some will find it necessary to write requesting credit. Say the standard application form does not convey a true picture of you. If, for example, you are young and applying for credit for the first time, your qualifications as presented on the application may not suffice. A letter in which you explain your excellent prospects could help.

Most forms ask for credit references. Good credit references mean a lot, particularly if you do not have a large savings account or a hefty salary. If you have never bought on credit, however, you won't have any credit references. In this case, a letter explaining how you always purchase for cash can help you get the credit.

A woman who through divorce or death is suddenly single can have trouble establishing credit in her own name if everything has been in her husband's name. In this case, a letter of explanation is necessary.

In the first sample, a woman has recently received a degree and moved to a new town. Since she is new in the community, on her first job, and with no prior credit history, a letter giving some positive details and accomplishments can help.

Credit Manager
National Bank
Main Street
City, State zip

Dear Credit Manager:

I am applying for your bank's credit card.

I recently moved to this city after earning my doctorate in chemistry cum laude. I have been hired as a junior research chemist by ABC Chemical.

My doctoral dissertation is being published next year by Professional & Reference Book Publishers in New York.

Although I have no prior credit history, I believe my prospects are excellent and I would be a valuable credit card user. I would like a card at this time for its convenience. I am paid monthly and having a credit card would allow me to pay monthly for purchases.

Thank you for your consideration.

In the sample that follows, an individual has never bought on credit.

Credit Card Manager
Big Bank
High Street
City, State zip

Dear Manager:

For business reasons, I would like to apply for your Super Credit Card. Having this card would make it easier for me to keep track of business expenses for reimbursement and for tax purposes.

This will be my first such card. Heretofore, I have made cash purchases only, even of such items as a car. Since I do not own a home, I have no mortgage. I believe that my ability to pay cash indicates I am a good credit risk despite having no credit history. As my application shows, I have a modest savings account and some bonds.

Sincerely,

In the next sample, a woman has to explain her lack of a credit history.

Dear Credit Manager:

I am eager to open a charge account with your department store in my own name. As my application shows, I have an excellent job, modest savings, and equity in a house. I have, however, no previous credit history. That is because everything was in my former husband's name. During our marriage, however, I paid half of all our expenses.

Your records will indicate that my former husband and I had an account with your store for several years, which I used mostly, although it was in his name. You will see that I was a good customer.

Thank you for your help on this.

Sincerely,

"I CAN'T PAY" LETTERS

As noted in Chapter 2, the "I can't pay" letter is a case of having to put a negative message in positive terms. Since the essence of effective writing is being positive, this is an especially important point to remember. Do not say, "I can't pay." Say when you *can* pay.

> Manager
> Action Collection Agency
> Northeast Street
> City, State zip
>
> Dear Sir,
>
> In response to your letter, I would like to make arrangements to pay $40 a month on my outstanding debt. I will mail the amount to you no later than the 5th of each month.
>
> I hope this is satisfactory to you. I am eager to wipe out this debt as quickly as my circumstances permit. Thank you for your help on this.

CREDIT CARD LETTERS

A letter that even the most confirmed nonwriter is sometimes forced to write pertains to credit cards. Not to obtain one, which is treated in the previous section. This need, unfortunately, is to straighten out a billing error that repeated calls have failed to correct.

In a sense these are letters offering and seeking information as well as requesting action. Many large department stores or credit card companies put an address on their bill to which you can write with questions. Most also give you a statement of procedures to follow in case of error when you first open an account. File that in a safe place for future use.

TIP: Timeliness is important when writing about a billing error. Many companies require notification of a possible error after no more than 60 days. Writing later could jeopardize your claim.

The store must respond within 30 days and take some action within 90 days.

Your letter should include:

- Your name, address, and account number (telephone number optional)
- The dollar amount of the perceived error
- Description of the error and, if possible, why you believe it is an error

In regard to the last item, if you cannot explain your reasons, you might request an explanation of why the amount is what it is.

Use a business letter format, as below. Keep your approach straightforward and, as a rule, do not get huffy.

Dear Credit Manager:

RE: Thomas Burgess Account No. 11221122

My last bill (Nov 1) erroneously charges $334.56 to me for a clothes dryer.

Apparently, the branch store where I shop failed to notify your billing department that I had canceled the order.

I trust this will be corrected on my next bill.

Thank you.

Sometimes you do want to get huffy, if the business organization you have been dealing with has been unresponsive. Consider the following:

Credit Manager
Jade Mason Dept Store
333 Main Blvd
Boston, MA 33333

Dear Credit Manager:

Apparently your department has opened two accounts for me.

At least it has sent me two credit cards, each with a different account number and each with a different spelling of my name—neither correct.

I suppose the second account was opened after I notified your department of the misspelling of my name in the first account.

Thank you for opening a second account for me, but I would rather have my name spelled correctly in one account than wrong in two accounts.

The easiest way to solve the problem at this point is to cancel both accounts. Enclosed you will find the credit cards you sent me, destroyed.

Yours,

LETTERS SEEKING INFORMATION

Letters seeking information can be for a huge variety of topics: a company's product, plane schedules, how to file a claim, or even such mundane matters as garbage collection routes. Writing for a catalog is a request for information also. All such requests share the same qualities of simplicity, directness, and brevity.

Do not include unnecessary information. Use paragraphs and, if it seems appropriate, mechanical devices (spaces, numbered lists), to organize your request for the reader's convenience. Being organized and clear will speed the handling of your request.

This is not a letter of persuasion. In most cases it will be a first step in establishing a business relationship, and the reader will want to be prompt and helpful. You do not need to convince him or her to do what you ask. A businesslike statement of your needs and what you want from the reader will be sufficient.

Dear Sir or Madam:

I am interested in applying to Brown University for admission as a transfer student in the fall of 1988.

Please forward the necessary forms and information, including a complete course catalogue.

After receiving these materials, I will call to arrange a campus visit and interview.

Thank you for your assistance. I look forward to hearing from you.

NJB Instruments
1234 Upper Elm
Music City, OH

To whom it may concern:

I am a musician and I regularly use your products in my recording and live performances. I have had some difficulty, however, locating a retailer in my area who carries your complete line.

Would you please send me a list of the stores that stock your instruments and accessories in the Middletown region? Please also send information about buying directly from your factory by mail, in case there are no stores nearby.

Thank you.

Springfield Cultural Center
1 Main Street
Springfield, State

Dear SCC:

Please send a schedule of events for the fall season to me at the above address. I have recently moved to the area and am interested in cultural activities open to the public.

Would you please also send information about membership in the Center?

Thank you very much.

LETTERS OF COMPLAINT

Complaint letters, as noted in Chapter 2, can do one of two things: They can seek to remedy the mistake, or they can simply express your feelings. Decide, *before* you send a letter of complaint, which you wish to do.

If you want to persuade the reader to fix the mistake, be persuasive. In general, this means being positive. Don't sound angry, offensive, or petulant. These attitudes can make you sound ineffectual or childish. They turn people off in person, and in writing they are easier to dismiss—by throwing your letter in the wastebasket!

State your complaint calmly and clearly, then state precisely what you think ought to be done about it. You don't necessarily have to tell the reader what to do. Just make it clear that you expect corrective action to be taken.

In this sort of letter clarity, conciseness, and directness are very important. Any rational person reading the letter will at the very least be persuaded that your complaint is reasonable and will want to mend matters. If the response you get is *not* reasonable, then it's time for the second kind of complaint.

The blowing-off-steam letter is usually not aimed at producing action. It might at best elicit an apology. It is written when you are beyond the point of expecting or even wanting anything from the company—you just want to let them know that they've lost one valuable customer. Even so, there are points to keep in mind, to avoid sounding childish, shrill, and possibly even wrong:

- Organize your thoughts so that the letter is coherent. (A chaotic burst of accusations will not be as effective as a well-reasoned presentation.)

- Don't bring up irrelevant issues. (This distracts from the point you are trying to make.)

- Avoid personal attacks. (Personality is only relevant if it directly relates to your case—a rude salesperson, for example.)

- Begin with the main object of your complaint or with a statement of what you intend to do. (If you are canceling your account, this is a sure attention getter.)

- Close with a reiteration of why you feel justified in complaining.

The Please-Take-Action Complaint

To whom it may concern:

Enclosed please find one copy of the record "Greenback Dollar" that I ordered from your catalog last month.

The record contains numerous scratches and was already opened when I received it.

I would like to request a replacement copy of the same record. If that album is not available, I would like a refund.

Thank you.

A Sharper Complaint Letter

I am writing to request action on a mishandled order that has been delayed for more than 5 months.

On July 12 I sent in a form clipped from your magazine, requesting a subscription at the introductory fee of 12 months for the price of 10. I included a check for $23.95 (a copy of the canceled check is enclosed). The form indicated that the subscription would begin immediately.

On October 5, I still had not received a single issue, although I *had* received the canceled check, which apparently you had cashed. I wrote and requested that delivery begin immediately, and received an apology and a promise that the next issue of Zip Code World would arrive within 2 weeks. Copies of both letters are enclosed.

On November 12 the magazine still had not arrived, although by now I had begun receiving notices to renew my subscription! A bill arrived for the first year's subscription, *at the normal price,* rather than the special introductory price.

I have now been billed twice for magazines I have not yet received. At this point I am giving you an option: either return my money to me *in full,* or deliver the magazine (current and back issues) immediately upon receipt of this letter. I am rapidly losing my patience.

A Blowing-Off-Steam Letter

Credit Manager
L&M Dept. Stores
New London, CT 06320

Dear Sir:

I have today instructed your store to cancel my account and have stopped the purchase of an ordered dishwasher.

While I rarely take the time to write letters of complaint, I am sufficiently angry to make an exception in your case.

We have shopped at L&M ever since we came to the area in 1961. In the course of nearly 18 years we have made many purchases, including a washing machine, a dryer, two vacuum cleaners, stereo equipment, two dishwashers, various tools and small appliances (radial arm saw, clocks, radios, etc.), household goods (rugs, bedding, etc.), automotive equipment, clothes, furniture, etc., etc., etc.

Your records, and you apparently keep very good records, will document these purchases. If you are interested, you might just look.

I have canceled my account because my wife and I have been hassled, dunned, and treated with a CIA-like scrutiny that has finally and emphatically convinced me that L&M has been in a highly reluctant relationship with us. It is precisely this relationship of reluctant beneficence that I joyously discontinue, along with my account.

A copy of this letter will be sent to your main office.

Very sincerely,

For additional samples of complaint writing, see Chapter 2.

PLACING ORDERS

Order letters are very straightforward. You don't have to worry about sounding sincere, sympathetic, or interested. In fact, the less you say the better. But always remember to include these things: *what* you want, *how many,* size, color, any other necessary descriptive information, the *price* if you know it, a catalog number if you have one, your name and address, and the date (as with all letters).

Make the request as orderly as possible, so the reader will quickly see what you want. If you know the cost of the item you are ordering, and you know that the firm is reliable, enclose a check with the order; this will facilitate matters.

Credit Manager
Zip Code Thinkers Corporation
889 Limited Access Highway
Jacksonville, FL 32245-7157

To whom it may concern:

Please forward to my attention an application for credit and your most recent catalog. We are interested in establishing an open 30-day wholesale account with your company.

Please find enclosed check #22320 in the amount of $22 to cover the cost of both the catalog and a 1-year subscription to What's New in Zip Codes magazine.

Thank you.

Farbe Pen Co.
1210 Jackson St.
North East, PA 18766

To whom it may concern:

I would like to order 12 dozen medium-point blue ball point pens and 12 dozen green felt-tip markers. The catalog numbers are 12776 and 12539, respectively.

The prices are listed at $0.99/doz. for the ball point pens and $1.15/doz. for the markers, when ordering over 7 dozen. I have enclosed a check for $27.47 to cover the cost of the order, including 7% sales tax.

Please ship to my attention at the above address. Thank you.

Orders may also be written as simple memos, which allow you to present the information in a visually clear and concise manner. This is probably the only time you would use a memo format outside of interoffice business mail.

TO: Ihren Klang Bagpipes Ltd.

FROM: Connecticut Valley Pipers Ass'n.

SUBJECT: Order No. 11777

Please ship four new bagpipes to CVPA immediately and charge them to our account, #4703.

Thank you.

WRITING TO CONGRESS

Letters to Congress are usually for a very specific purpose. You write to urge your congressperson to vote for or against a particular bill. You can also write to say you approve or disapprove of a vote or a position the representative has taken. You can also write for information.

Most letters are read by aides, not by the representative or senator. You may want to present an argument to support your view, but if you do, keep it direct and avoid too much detail. Your letters will be considered primarily on the basis of which view you support, not how thoroughly you defend it—so write to the point.

Your representative's or senator's opinion will be swayed as much—or more—by the fact that you have written, as by how well you argue your point. Nonetheless, be careful in your presentation. Also, avoid the angry tone. It doesn't convince, and it will detract from what you are saying.

If you have been a supporter of the congressperson in the past, say so, whether or not you agree with his or her position on the issue in question. Elected officials are very sensitive to their constituents' views and are responsive to someone they know has voted for them in the past.

If you have voted against the congressperson, don't say so. Your opinion won't hold much weight, since he or she won't be counting on your vote anyway. Of course, if you have decided, based on some action taken since the election, to vote for him or her, mention that. If you are undecided, and the issue you are writing about is going to make a difference in your decision, say so.

Finally, if you know the number of the bill you are writing to ' upport, include that in your letter. It will help the staff sort it quickly and will prevent the letter from getting lost in the shuffle.

If you do not know your senator's or representative's address, you can address the letter to him or her care of the branch of Congress to which he or she belongs. The addresses given in the samples below are correct.

The Honorable Joseph P. Smothers
United States Senate
Washington, DC 20510

Dear Senator Smothers:

I am writing to urge you to vote in favor of Senate Bill 133, which would require all foods that have been irradiated as a preservative measure to be clearly marked as such when sold to the public.

Since the health effects of irradiation are as yet unclear, it is only fair that consumers should be aware when they are buying food that has been treated in this manner.

In view of your past support of consumer rights, I am confident you will see the justice in this effort to protect and inform the public. Once again, I urge you to vote yes on Senate Bill 133.

The Honorable Jane C. Ellis
House of Representatives
Washington, DC 20515

Dear Ms. Ellis:

I am writing because I have long supported your stand on

U.S. foreign policy, and I want to urge you to continue in your courageous defense of reason and moderation, in the face of often ferocious and irrational opposition.

We live in a time when ill-considered, hasty, or selfish actions can have truly horrifying consequences for the entire world. It is absolutely essential that people in responsible positions be able to maintain a calm and balanced view of our interests and those of world peace. Your actions in your 5 years in Congress have demonstrated that you have done just that.

Bravo, Ms. Ellis! I and hundreds of others in District 12 stand behind you. Keep up the good work.

The Honorable Nathan Wise
House of Representatives
Washington, DC 20515

Dear Mr. Wise:

I have voted for you in every election for the past 9 years. One of my main reasons for voting for you has been your vocal commitment to the environment and the health of your constituents.

It was therefore with dismay that I learned of your support for HR 237, which would allow the production and sale of genetically altered organisms for use outside the laboratory.

This matter may seem small now, and "experts" may say they know such sales are safe. But this bill will start us on a slippery slope toward a time when indiscriminate use of genetic engineering may well endanger our entire ecosystem. The experts have been wrong before. This kind of work will affect the entire life cycle on an unprecedented scale. Much more work needs to be done before we can truly say that it is safe to use genetic engineering in the environment.

In the name of caution, and in light of your own record of environmental awareness, I strongly encourage you to oppose HR 237.

You can also write to your congressperson for information. This can be information about a particular bill—when it is going to be voted on, what committee is handling it, who is sponsoring it, what lobbies are supporting or opposing it, and what your representative's position is.

You can write to request copies of a bill, government publications (or lists of them, if you don't know what to ask for), or for information about some point of interest.

Your congressional office can do much for you, and the best way to find out if it can help you is to ask. Again, keep the letter brief and to the point. Asking for too much at once may slow down the response time.

Dear Mr. Abramson:

I am a biotechnology researcher working on experimental pesticides for a major chemical manufacturing firm. I need your help in locating current laws and regulations governing the use of genetically altered organisms outside the laboratory.

Can you provide me with a list of current rulings and regulations in this field? If you can also provide a list of current and pending legislation that deals with this topic, I would be most grateful.

You may reply to me care of [name and address of company].

Thank you for your assistance.

TIP: You can write to any federal government agency for information. The federal government is probably the largest publisher in the world. For a list of its publications, which cover a large variety of topics and are usually free, write to the Superintendent of Documents, U.S. Government Printing Office (GPO), Washington, D.C. 20402. Two very useful publications are the *U.S. Government Printing Office Style Manual* and the *Congressional Directory*. The latter gives names, addresses, and titles of all key officials.

LETTERS TO THE EDITOR

A few people write letters to the editor merely to see their words and name in print. It is an ego trip for such people, who write frequently to the newspaper. After a while, editors limit the number of letters they will print from one person and even stop printing them altogether.

If you are like most people, however, you write letters to the editor when you feel strongly about a topic of current interest. Two particular motives trigger most letters to the editor: (1) to correct an error, and (2) to convince readers to accept a particular point of view.

Whatever the motivation, such letters, unlike any others you write, aim at a large audience—everyone who reads the paper or magazine to which you write. It is an opportunity to present yourself in a good or bad light to a maximum number of people—which light is entirely up to you and your writing skills.

Present your best self in your letter. Diatribes and jeremiads, even if they do make it into print, are usually just laughed at. If your letter is angry, make sure that it is well thought out, clearly presented, intelligently argued. The most important rule to follow when you are writing for publication is:

REREAD AND REVISE—AND THEN DO IT AT LEAST
ONE MORE TIME.

Letters to the editor are those rare ones in which you *avoid* the "you" approach. You are writing to the community at large, not to any one individual or group. You may at times direct your comments to the editor of the paper in question, which is the only situation where it may be appropriate to use "you."

Sometimes letters will address another letter writer, to whom they are replying, with "you." It may seem like an effective rhetorical device, but nine times out of ten it makes the writer look amateurish and uneducated. The accepted form is to refer to the other writer in the third person; this makes it clear that you are speaking to the community as a whole, which constitutes 99 percent of your readership.

Since you are trying to persuade, speak positively, support your argument with specifics, stick to the point, and keep it short. Most newspapers and magazines have a word limit because space is short. Do not waste space with emotional outbursts and personal attacks. Your letter should not be unfeeling, but it should show the reader why your powerful emotional reaction—joy, rage, sorrow—is the only possible reaction a thinking, feeling person could have.

TIP: Most publications have rules for the format and length of letters—usually typed, double-spaced, and no more than 300 words. They require your name, address, and telephone number be clearly visible. You *must* follow these rules. The telephone number is important because before publishing it, most papers will call you to confirm it was really you who wrote the letter. Look for the rules on the editorial or letter-to-the-editor page and *follow them!*

Letters may be about some local, immediate issue—whether to put a traffic light on a particular corner—or they may deal with international issues of life and death. They may share an experience or an emotion; they may urge action (support for a bill or candidate or a cause); they may simply express an opinion. In each case they are one of the most important ways you have of participating in the free exchange of ideas that characterizes a true democracy.

The following examples were taken (in some cases modified) from the editorial pages of actual newspapers.

A personal reaction to a public event:

To the Editor:

Since the loss of the Challenger and its crew, I have been haunted by John Donne's "No man is an island, entire of itself....Any man's death diminishes me...." This feeling was very real at the time of the assassinations of John Kennedy, Robert Kennedy, and Martin Luther King, Jr., but I experienced it even more profoundly at the death of Christa McAuliffe.

Christa was a common person and a social studies teacher; I am a common person and a social studies teacher. She went while I was afraid to apply. A piece of me and every other teacher went with her aboard Challenger. All Americans grieve for the loss of seven of our finest, one of whom happened to be a teacher.

I hope we will do more than grieve. Because of her life and

daring, I feel inspired to work harder at my job; she makes me proud to be a teacher. But further I hope that our most talented and gifted youth will choose to follow her. They do not have to go into space to do so; they need to follow the example of her life and consider teaching as a career. I believe Christa's desire to challenge people to become teachers was one reason she dared put her life on the line. [Modified, based on a letter to *The Day*, New London, Connecticut.]

An opinion on a matter of national policy:

To the Editor:

At the same time that Libyan civilians were counting their dead and assessing the damage inflicted by the early-morning bombings of April 15, Americans from Bangor to San Francisco were talking proudly of justice and honor. Libya's Col. Muammar el-Qaddafi committed a crime, they said, and he deserved to be punished.

"The Terrorist and His Sentence," you called it (editorial, April 15). Americans can assuage any moral reservations they might have with what you term "the sober satisfaction of seeing justice done."

Hospital beds filled with bloodied children are a strange definition of justice. Streets strewn with the rubble of bombed apartment buildings are a strange definition of justice. And the death of Colonel Qaddafi's infant daughter is a strange definition of justice. I suggest that these tragic sights have nothing to do with justice, but instead define a narrowing of the moral gulf that separates Colonel Qaddafi and the United States.

Nietzsche once warned that "whoever battles with monsters had better see that it does not turn him into a monster." We would do well to heed that warning. [Mark O. Hatfield, U.S. Senator from Oregon, in the *New York Times*, Sunday, April 20, 1986.]

A letter on a local matter, in response to a previous editorial:

To the Editor:

I am writing to thank the editorial staff of the *Day* for its complimentary editorial of June 24, recognizing me and two other area women for our work in the community.

However, although I was very supportive of the graduation ceremony at Norris Correctional Institution, my part basically consisted of arranging for publicity, which the *Day* provided, and obtaining corsages through the generosity of a State Prison Association volunteer sponsor, Mary Pacheco.

It was through the quiet, patient, and persevering efforts of Betty Oriso, a teacher at Norris, who, with her fellow teachers, not only encouraged her students to obtain their diplomas but gained approval of the graduation exercises through the Department of Corrections and arranged every detail of the ceremony, that the whole thing was made possible.

My brief role "behind-the-scene" of this celebration may have been more visible than the real "behind-the-scene" work and dedication of Betty Oriso, another local woman working to improve life in our community. [Modified, based on a letter to *The Day*, New London, Connecticut, Saturday, June 28, 1986.]

COLLEGE APPLICATION ESSAYS

Most colleges require an essay in which applicants discuss matters that do not show up elsewhere on the application form. The essay helps the college get to know them better and evaluate their writing skills.

The most common essay is simply an autobiography. The school asks for information about your strengths and weaknesses, interests, personality, and your education—both formal and informal. Such an essay is difficult to write because we often cannot see ourselves clearly. The essay can help you give an objective evaluation of your own performance and understand yourself better.

Clarity, conciseness (there is usually a length limit), good organization, and knowing what you want to say are essential. The skills demanded by this essay will be useful throughout life, in self-evaluations for employers, and in analyzing your wants when making career decisions or changes.

If you are just getting out of high school when you write this essay, you may feel you do not have a lot of experience to talk about in your essay. This is probably not true. First of all, remember to talk about your *interests,* why you are applying to college.

Colleges want applicants who are curious and eager to learn. So if you are interested in computer science, for example, say so, even if you don't have much experience in the field. Then say what you do have—you may be surprised! Perhaps you read magazine articles regularly, took a course in school, joined a club or users' group. All these count in your favor.

Similarly, suppose you like to draw, or write short stories. Even if you have never tried to do anything with your work—get it published, have it exhibited in school—the college wants to know about your interest. Of course, if you do have evidence of your accomplishments—trophies, a record of your service as officer of a club—by all means mention them as well.

Try to offer a fair analysis of your weaknesses and strengths. If you tend to be too hard on yourself, practice painting a more objective—and attractive!—portrait, both for others and for yourself. If, on the other hand, you have a habit of boasting, try to present as realistic a sense of your weaknesses as you do of your strengths. Don't make promises you can't keep.

Strengths and weaknesses do not refer only to academic skills, and most colleges prefer that you don't limit yourself to that area. How well you get along with others, your leadership abilities, your self-discipline and ability to plan, your concerns about society, your career or other life plans—all are valid topics to cover in the essay.

Explain why you think you are strong in a particular area or why you feel a need to improve. This can be done positively. Let's say you need to improve your self-discipline and study habits. Don't just say, "I have poor study habits." Self-discipline is an important life skill, so talk about it in that way. Show how your desire to improve this skill relates to your college plans.

The essay generally covers two themes, which can be treated separately or together:

1. A description of some of your more important interests, hobbies, activities, and accomplishments (the "externals")

2. An analysis of your personality as it relates to school— how you get along with people, your academic skills, your strengths and weaknesses

I will graduate from high school in June of next year. As can be seen from my transcript, I maintained a B average in all classes except Chemistry.

In high school I have been a member of the swimming team, the debating club, and the varsity cheerleader squad. My senior year I was elected president of the debating club.

I have many interests outside school, both academic and social. I am interested in local politics, which I follow in the newspapers, and in animal welfare. I belong to a community group active in promoting concern for animals. In the summer between my junior and senior years I worked evenings backstage on a community theater production of "The Glass Menagerie," helping with sets and costumes. During the day I worked as a cashier at a local department store.

I have been asked to assess what I can contribute to the college community. I believe that my leadership ability is one of my strongest assets. I have often been told that I am very good at getting people to cooperate, without being egotistical or power hungry. I also believe that my concern for society as a whole is an asset.

On the negative side, I am somewhat disorganized, which keeps me from functioning at peak efficiency—although when the pressure's on, I know how to keep my nose to the grindstone! I look forward to the challenge of college.

I sincerely hope to be admitted to Central University and am eager to take advantage of the superior academic opportunities it has to offer. I look forward to answering any further questions you may have at our upcoming interview.

If you have been out of school for a while, you will probably have more to say about yourself and your experience. This is good and bad: Experience is always an asset, but now you have to condense and eliminate even more.

I graduated from high school 4 years ago. Since that time, I have served 2 years in the armed forces (Navy), and I have worked at many jobs, including bus driver, library aide, dishwasher, and bookkeeper. Many of these jobs were part-time and/or temporary, and I often held two jobs at once.

In the Navy I was introduced to basic bookkeeping techniques. I don't really like the work, but it is a useful source of income when I can't find any other work. I also learned self-discipline and routine in the service. I can apply myself to any task, even one I hate, and keep at it until it is finished. I think this will be a particular advantage for me in returning to school, since my study habits in high school were not very good.

Teachers and friends have told me I would make a good writer. I have a sense of humor and know how to tell a story. My teachers said I had strong English writing skills. This is why I am interested in majoring in journalism. I have included a letter of recommendation from my senior English teacher, Mr. Duval.

I feel that my major assets are my ability to work and my ability as a writer. In addition, I am an easygoing, tolerant person, so I won't have any trouble getting along with my classmates. My weaknesses are that I don't often stick with any one thing very long. I'll do what needs doing, but when that's over, I leave it and go on to something else. I hope to get into journalism a little more deeply than that, because I would like to make a career of it.

Please give my application your serious consideration. I believe I have something to offer your college, because of my age and experience. I know that the college has a great deal to offer me, and I hope to be able to take advantage of that.

MINUTES OF THE MEETING

Minutes are an important record of the proceedings of any club or organization. They include:

1. Date, time, location, and presiding officer

2. Attending members

3. Approval of previous minutes and of treasurer's report

4. Business left unfinished at the last meeting and continued at this one

5. Summary of reports

6. New business

7. Committee appointments

8. Election of officers

9. Adjournment time

Set off the name of the group, the date, and the kind of meeting from the body of the minutes. Include in the first paragraph the date, time, place, and presiding officer. List names of attendees alphabetically. If all but a few members are present, you can save space by saying, "All members were present except..." and list alphabetically those members who were absent.

Minutes of a noncommercial, community-access radio station staff meeting:

WXYZ STAFF MEETING
October 15

The WXYZ staff meeting was called to order on Wednesday, October 15, at 7 p.m. by Andrew Lord, operations manager. Attending were [names of attendees or "Absent were...."]

Minutes of the previous meeting (September 15) were approved without correction. No treasurer's report was scheduled.

The Operations Board chair, Cinnara Jackson, presented the Operations Board report (attached). The only item requiring action was the vacant position of director of development.

Lucy Ciel nominated Fred Jones for the position, Philip Young seconded, and he was elected by a voice vote.

The program director, Leonora Billings, reported on recent FCC rulings and federal court decisions regarding the broadcast of "obscene, indecent, or profane" material. Phil Viczenczy noted that there has been a problem with some of the deejays ignoring WXYZ station policy on this matter. He moved that "random checks of air sound be conducted at least three times a week and that violators be punished according to policy."

A heated discussion followed this motion. Some people felt it was censorship. Others argued that the regulations had been imposed; WXYZ was merely protecting itself from prosecution by the FCC. After an hour and a half of debate, Andrew Lord moved that the motion be tabled until the next staff meeting. The motion was accepted.

As there was no further business to discuss, the meeting was adjourned at 9:30 p.m.

The Jerusalem County Historical Society Monthly Meeting, May 1

The monthly meeting of the Jerusalem County Historical Society was called to order by Caroline Lorschetsky, president, Friday, May 1, at 11 a.m.

A quorum was present as all members were in attendance except Elizabeth Balfour, Levon Burton, Joanne Davidson, and David Hutton.

Copies of the minutes of the April 2 meeting were distributed and approved.

Copies of the treasurer's report were distributed and approved.

Fund-raising Committee Report
Chair of the Fund-raising Committee, Albert Wong, reported that subscriptions to the newsletter *Older and Better!* had increased this year by about 5 percent and that a subcommittee was being formed to set up a new subscription drive. He

also reported on progress on the Festival being planned at the Ulafson House in July. Two local musicians so far have agreed to donate their services, several food concessions have already been rented, and admissions tickets and raffle tickets are being designed by the artist, Alice Webster. Several members volunteered to help out on the day of the Festival.

No new motions or other business were offered. The meeting adjourned at 1:15 p.m.

SUMMING UP

In every life a time will arise when writing for action becomes necessary. When that happens to you, act. Write. Do not delay. No task has ever become easier by being postponed. If you get right at it, think about the point or points you need to make, and use the guidelines and samples in this book, not only will you find the job easier than you expected, but you will take pride in the result. And, most important, you will trigger the action you desire.

Think about what you want to say. Say it, and only it, in a style that reflects your personality. And regardless of your emotional state, keep cool. Remember, as the old Chinese maxim has it: The palest ink is bolder than the loudest word.

11

Writing for a Job

Writing for a job is something nearly everyone has to do at one time or another, and it is probably the most important, demanding writing most people will ever do. A letter seeking a job is a selling letter, a persuasion letter. It is particularly difficult for many people because they are trying to sell themselves and their skills. They may be shy. They may have difficulty talking about themselves—particularly in writing. They may be inarticulate and unable to convey well the extent of the skills that they really possess.

The most common form of job writing is the résumé. A résumé is a very special kind of writing. It sums up your experiences, describes your skills, and, if it is a good one, conveys to the reader what you can do for them. Fortunately, standardized formats for résumés make writing them easier. Below are some samples to guide you (check job-hunting books for other examples), as well as samples of different types of letters you most often must write in any serious job-hunting campaign.

RÉSUMÉ

The chief purpose of a résumé is to give an employer a profile of yourself by listing past jobs, education, and any information about yourself related to the particular job you want. It is not a letter and so does not require the same approach to style that most letters do.

Essentially, the résumé is a list presented in a set format. It does not conform to the rules of grammar or punctuation that a letter must obey. There are a number of possible layouts for a résumé; two of the most common are described and illustrated here.

Always put your name, address, and phone number at the top of the page, either in the left corner or in the center.

All résumés cover the same categories of information. These general categories and the order in which they usually appear are:

- Career objective
- Work experience
- Education
- References

Career Objective

Your career objective goes at the top of the résumé, after your address but before the list of your work experience. This helps the employer identify your goals. It also shows that you are looking ahead. One or two sentences suffice.

Work Experience

This is the bulk of the résumé. Two formats are widely used. Each has a slightly different emphasis. One is the reverse chronological list, and the other is a grouping of work experience by skills or tasks performed, giving important tasks first. The former is the more usual, especially for relatively new or obvious jobs. The latter is useful particularly if job titles do not quickly convey the essence of the skills required.

Reverse Chronological List

List your previous jobs by date with the last or current job first, second most recent job next, and so on. Give the name and address of the company you worked for, the dates you worked, and a brief description of your duties.

If you held a job for 2 years or more, give the years you were employed. If you had the job for fewer than 2 years, include months as well as years in the dates. If you have a long work history, instead of listing jobs by date, simply list the important ones first and group the unimportant ones at the end.

Do not list part-time or temporary jobs, unless you are just starting and have no other work experience.

Work Experience Listed by Tasks

List your experience in terms of the tasks you have performed and the skills required, in order of their importance, without mentioning the job in which you used them. Follow this with a list of your jobs, giving only the name, address, and phone number of the company for which you worked (still in reverse chronological order). The advantage of this format is that it highlights your skills, some of which may not have been in use in your most recent job.

Education

List your education in reverse chronological order. Include only high schools, colleges, and business or technical schools. Do not list elementary schools. Give the number of years of high school completed (e.g., 1, 2, 3, 4). Include the diploma or degree you received at college. State your major subject and minor subject, if any.

If you have taken any relevant courses outside the schools listed, mention them (e.g., Principles of Accounting, Effective Speaking).

List any honors you have received during your education (e.g., Honor Society, Phi Beta Kappa, Valedictorian, Boys or Girls State). Modesty ill becomes the writing of a résumé.

Professional and Business Associations

This section is optional. If you are a member of professional and business associations, include them. List them in the order of their importance to you. If you have recently graduated from high school or college, include extracurricular activities and clubs. State any offices you held.

References

Give the names of three or four people who know you. Try to include someone you have worked for as well as someone who knows you socially. Do not list relatives. Get permission from the people whose names you do use and tell them you plan to put their names, addresses, and phone numbers on your résumé.

Another option is to say on your résumé that references will be supplied upon request. This eliminates the need to list names, addresses, and telephone numbers except for serious job proposals. You should of course be prepared to supply the list of references when asked.

Optional Summary Element

Some résumés include a brief paragraph at the beginning that summarizes career highlights and significant accomplishments. This is an especially valuable addition for people who have considerable experience and expertise in a particular field.

You need not restrict the opening summary to experience or expertise gained from a salaried job. You can list accomplishments in community organizations, hobbies, and other unpaid activities. The criterion for including them is their relevance to your career objective or to the job for which you are applying.

Résumé Pointers

Below are seven points to remember when putting together your résumé.

- Avoid giving personal information unless it pertains to the work you are going to do.

- It is against the law for employers to request information about age, sex, religious preference, ethnic background, or political beliefs.

- It is acceptable, but not necessary, to indicate your marital or military status.

- A photograph, once considered a useful addition to the résumé, is no longer advised because it is a nonverbal way of communicating unnecessary personal information.

- Do not add any unnecessary material to your résumé. Most employers are definitely not interested in personal matters if they do not affect your work.

- Do not discuss salaries in your résumé. You can deal with this in the interview. Listing a particular salary makes it difficult to bargain later. Always leave the question open.

- Do not say why you left your last job. There are various reasons why you may have been laid off: work slowdown, job discontinued, business dissolved, cutback for economic reasons, and so on. Most employers will not hold these problems against you. If you have quit, it could have been because of dissatisfaction, minor health problems, or other acceptable reasons. This can be discussed at the interview.

Résumé Preparation

You can type a small number of résumés yourself, but if you wish to contact a lot of companies, have your résumé printed by a professional printer. This is relatively inexpensive, and printing will save you a great deal of work, especially if you are not a good typist.

If you have access to a word processor, it can be a quick way to produce a lot of résumés cheaply—more than you would want to type by hand, but fewer than it would be worth having printed.

Use a word processor if at all possible to prepare your résumé. Once it is on a word processor, you can change the format, update it, or tailor it to a specific job easily without redoing the whole thing.

Organization Counts

Good organization is the keystone for your résumé. A well-written résumé tells the employer something about you before he or she has even judged your job experience: that you are a well-organized, neat, clear thinker. A résumé prepared with care tells the employer how determined and sincere you are in your ambitions and goals.

Sample Résumés

Jill Jones
103 Ortega St.
San Francisco, CA 92116
Phone

OBJECTIVE:

Fund-raising for nonprofit organization, preferably with opportunity for managing fund-raising campaign.

EXPERIENCE:

1987–1989
Supervisor/Director, Telemarketing Concepts, Berkeley, CA.

Directed four telephone fund-raising campaigns—for a political party, an environmental organization, a local candidate, and a ballot initiative campaign. Supervised phone bank workers and developed fund-raising strategies, working with campaign coordinators and liaisons.

1985–1987
Tour Coordinator, Poetry Players, El Cerrito, CA.

Booked performances by educational theatre company, singly and in groups, with schools, libraries, senior citizen and community centers throughout Northern California and Oregon. This included selling the shows and coordinating performance dates. Handled all logistical requirements (motels, transportation, food, etc.) as well as actor contracts, performance contracts, correspondence and other secretarial duties.

1982–1985
Canvasser and Canvass Coordinator, Concerned Neighbors in Action, Oakland, CA.

Supervised canvass crews raising money for health care reform. Trained new crew members. Coordinated movements with other campaigns working the same territory, to avoid canvassing the same areas at the same time. Averaged $85/night as a canvasser.

EDUCATION:

Antioch College, BA, 1982.
Major: Political Science. Minor: Anthropology
Editor, campus literary magazine.
Laney College, Oakland, 1983–1984. Course in accounting.
UC Berkeley Extension, 1987–1988. Course in municipal government.

REFERENCES ON REQUEST

Notice how the writer has organized the résumé to highlight those aspects of her experience that further her career goal—in this case, fund-raising work. Potential employers will see that she also has a fair amount of managerial experience, but this is not something she has chosen to emphasize, except as it relates to her primary goal. If the position she is seeking were strictly supervising others, she could have written her résumé to stress that part of her work history. As it is, she presents a powerful array of skills that point in exactly the direction she wants to go.

Karen Gomez
32 Ultra Vista Ave.
San Bernardino, CA

POSITION SOUGHT:

Word Processing Operator

EXPERIENCE:

September 1988—present

Assistant sales correspondent. Value Insurance Co., 4331 Camino Real, Alameda, CA (phone). Supervisor: Ms. Anna Robinson.

September 1986—June 1988

Teller. Westwood Bank & Trust, 93 MacArthur Blvd., Oakland, CA (phone). Supervisor: Mr. Morris Blades.

EDUCATION:

Will graduate with a B average from Pilgrim High School in June 1989.

Participated in the Office Education Training Program in senior year. Specialized in business courses and attained:

1. Typing speed, 60 wpm; shorthand, 120 wpm.

2. Working knowledge of transcribing machines, IBM Personal Computers and Personal Systems, and all components of the Young Office Information System.

3. Skill with electronic calculators.

4. Excellent human relations skills in dealing with co-workers, superiors, and subordinates.

EXTRACURRICULAR ACTIVITIES

Member, Oakland Chapter of California Office Education Association

Member, California Chapter of Future Business Leaders of America

Chairperson, Future Business Leaders of America Fund-Raising Drive to raise $2,000 for activities

Swimming Team

Debating Team

School Newspaper Reporter

REFERENCES UPON REQUEST

Here is a person, fresh out of high school, who, although she does not have very much work experience, has put together a convincing résumé. She does not pad her work history; instead, she presents what she has done and focuses on her strengths, which in this case are educational. She talks about the courses she has taken, the skills she has acquired, and the organizations in which she has participated that have some relevance to her position goal. This last is important for someone with not much experience, because it suggests that she has group skills necessary for successful functioning in an office. Finally, she has presented a realistic goal for the résumé, which suggests that she is practical and able to work toward achievable goals.

Phyllis Philbrook
121 East 68th Street   Home Phone
New York, NY   Office Phone

EXPERIENCE

Over 7 years as acquiring editor in scientific and technical areas, including environmental science and engineering, energy, industrial safety and health.

Have managed the LNG and Goldberg & Thomas lists of biology titles, including reference books, monographs, texts and collections of historical papers. Representative titles include *Conservation of Inland Wetlands, Animals of the Great Lakes Regions, Marine Sources of Organic Fuels, The Role of Light in Evolution, Insects of North America.*

More than 14 presentations to sales staff and to company management describing new books and editorial plans.

Work with many authors on faculty of major universities and on technical, research, and engineering staffs in industry.

Attend numerous professional and academic association meetings to seek out new authors and to promote our books.

Good communication skills required to convince authors to publish with LNG and to convince product managers, other marketing staff, and management to publish new books I have recommended.

Four years' experience as a special projects editor at Eldridge Press. This included manuscript development for a college-level biology text requiring substantive editing, selecting photographs, overseeing preparation of all line art.

Knowledgeable about typesetting, copy editing, production, artwork preparation for scientific and technical books.

Familiar with promotion methods for scientific and technical books, including direct mail, space advertising, mailing list selection, catalog accounts, bookstore and professional association sales.

For 10 years was the editor (voluntary) for quarterly newsletter of Friends of the Earth, New York branch.

PLACES OF EMPLOYMENT

1985 to present
Long, North, & Greenhouse
Current title: Executive Editor

1981 to 1985
Moss & Wallace Book Company
Last title: Sponsoring Editor

1974 to 1981
Eldridge Press
Last title: Special Projects Editor

1971 to 1974
Lawford Book Company
Last title: Production Editor

October 1970 to March 1971
Museum of Modern Art
Assistant in Department of Public Relations

July 1969 to October 1970
Frick Art Reference Library
Assistant in Catalog and Print Order Departments

EDUCATION:

Smith College, Northampton, Mass.
B.A. in Art History in 1969
Junior year in Florence, Italy
Other Education: Presentation Skills Workshop
                   Managing for Results Workshop

OTHER INTERESTS: Tennis, cross-country skiing, biking, bird-
                   ing, gardening, wildflowers, pottery

This is an example of listing work experience by skills and tasks.
The writer's major skills are presented first, followed by a very concise list of employment in reverse chronological order.

   The writer of this résumé had to be very well organized, if only
because she had a lot of material to work with. She had to decide
how to present her years of experience in a concise yet representative summary. She has selected her strengths and briefly described
them so as to demonstrate why she would be a good choice for an
employer to make. Note also that the list is organized in terms of
the importance and generality of the tasks: It proceeds from most
important and most general (tasks that demand a combination of a
number of abilities) to the more specific and more peripheral.

Albert Sussman
P.O. Box 12121
Upton, NY

General management executive with very strong operations experience coupled with planning and negotiating skills gained at Computers Unlimited, National Natural Gas, and United Interstate.
Seasoned achiever of demanding company goals, especially in foreign business environments. Background spans operations, banking, marketing, and negotiating with the Department of Defense.

United Interstate Banks, Inc.   1984–present

Vice president—operations, Military Banking
Lyons, France (1988–present)

Accountable for 190-person department with annual budget of $7.5 million supporting a 120-branch retail banking network processing 100,000 average daily transactions. Line responsibility for Branch Services, Financial Control, DP Operations, Proof and Settlement, Systems Programming, Traffic, Communications, and Central Supply Departments. Concurrently managed 3-year modernization and automation program which achieved high-performance customer service. As a result, United Interstate Bank's profitability improved from a $4-million annual loss to a $2 million profit, the first profitability in the 15-year history of the bank.

- Successfully negotiated with the Department of International Banking Directorate and gained approval and budget authorization to implement a 3-year program which modernized a 120-branch retail banking network.

- Developed high-performance customer service delivery system, minimized paper handling, and facilitated introduction of new customer services that increased demand accounts and provided additional income.

- Recommended and achieved implementation of 30 automated teller machines (ATMs) throughout France. The ATMs are unique in the world, dispensing U.S. dollars and French currency, achieving approximately 5000 transactions monthly and increasing the Bank's demand deposit base.

- Introduced six decentralized branch automation minicomputers, resulting in faster branch balancing time and improved management information and control.

- Implemented improved retailed banking applications on new computer, avoiding $1 million redevelopment costs.

- Established a computer backup capability which reduced financial exposure in daily processing of $4 million of checks drawn on stateside banks.

- Instituted an overdraft checking service called "Bounce-less Checking" which generated $200,000 monthly service fee income.

- Managed $1.5 million program which significantly up-graded physical appearance of 55 branches.

- Contained overall head count to an increase of 5 positions while transaction volume increased 15 percent annually.

Director, Corporate Technology Review (1987–1988)

Responsible for a three-person management group with a budget of $600,000 monitoring the performance of worldwide data processing that represented a $195 million 1987 budget. Managed 6 to 10 system reviews annually of 8 to 10 major company data processing areas. Cost improvement recommendations, reflecting the performance reviews in 1987, were in excess of $1.25 million.

Developed performance management reporting system, in coordination with senior division representatives, used to monitor the monthly performance of software systems, business applications and computing resources of each divisional data processing center. Improved management controls resulted.

Director, MIS, International Division (1984–1986)

Directed 15-person systems staff with budget of $1.3 million. Initiated major program to revitalize outdated systems, including consolidating management control over geographically diverse business operations.

- Successfully implemented worldwide general ledger and information-reporting system with a 1-billion-character database. Also, implemented a "Forms of Value" and "Air Ticket" system resulting in savings of $200,000.

- Automated reporting for Mexico and implemented a program legalizing financial reporting for Worldwide Assistance operations in Italy.

- Managed European strategic study of the Worldwide Assistance Division which resulted in restructuring a data processing center in England which streamlined and upgraded management control.

National Natural Gas   1979–1983

Manager, Management Sciences Planning, International Division—
New York (1982–1983)

Staff manager responsible for monitoring the data processing activity of affiliates worldwide.

Reviewed the profit plans of International affiliates and provided cost improvement recommendations for action. Developed professional grading proposal which eliminated unnecessary grades while standardizing the remaining grades.

European EDP coordinator, England (1981–1982)

Coordinated data processing activities in 14 European countries. Directed 420 people and 370 installations in London, Paris, and Rome with a yearly budget of $9.2 million.

Operations Manager, International Gas Data Services, England (1979–1981)

Managed Operations Department of European Data Center serving units in England, Benelux, Scandinavia, Austria, and East Africa. Department consisted of a staff of 77, two IBM mainframes, one minicomputer, and related telecommunications equipment with a yearly budget of $1.4 million.

Computers Unlimited   1971–1978

Project Manager (1977–1978)

Research Analyst (1975–1977)

Instructor (1973–1975)

Technical Writer (1971–1973)

EDUCATION

EXCELL UNIVERSITY, Graduate School of Business, MBA Program in Executive Management

BLAKE UNIVERSITY, BA, 1970, Mathematics

PERSONAL

Born December 3, 1945; Married, two children. Fluent French.

This résumé begins, appropriately, with a general survey of the writer's experience and skills. Appropriately, because his experience is long and his skills are many, this summary gives the reader an idea of what he is all about without having to read the entire résumé. It is rather long, as résumés go, but in this case that is also appropriate.

Here a few statistics are very convincing, helping give a sense of the scope of some of his jobs. The writer wisely divides his work history into smaller sections on concrete accomplishments, as opposed to general skills or abilities. Not only does the physical format make the résumé easier to read, but the division into achievements also adds to the overall impression that this is a person who gets things done, the kind of person any corporation would be delighted to have on their team. Well-organized, attractively presented, and convincing—all in all, this is a high-powered résumé.

COVER LETTER

You will often be mailing your résumé to a prospective employer. When you do, you must include a brief letter with your résumé explaining why you are writing—either in response to an ad, which you should identify specifically, or because you are looking for a particular job that the company has to offer. In the letter you should repeat your career or job objectives, even if you have listed them on the résumé.

Keep your cover letter brief and to the point; your reader is undoubtedly very busy. Try to phrase your ideas in ways that will appeal to your prospective employer. Don't be clever; write about what you think will interest the employer, emphasizing those aspects of yourself that you think will be most attractive. Try to say what you can do for them. Write with their needs in mind. Above all, be courteous and sincere in your interest in the company.

Do be specific. If you can get information that might pertain to your job, try to use it to show your reader you are aware of her or his needs. If you know, for example, that the company specializes in a particular product or service, try to highlight in your letter how your skills can be used in that area.

Dear Sir or Madam:

In reply to your advertisement for a typist in today's *Times*, please accept this letter and the attached résumé as my application.

I graduated from high school last June, where I maintained a B+ average and had excellent secretarial experience. I have also worked as a typist in a business office under a cooperative work experience program.

My average net typing speed is 55 words per minute on 5-minute timed writings. I have worked for various teachers during the past year and have been the Typing Editor of the school yearbook. My shorthand speed is 100 words per minute.

I would very much appreciate the opportunity for a personal interview at your convenience.

Dear Ms. Alieri:

Please consider my application for the word processing vacancy advertised in the April 27 *Journal*. My enclosed résumé will, I believe, show that I have the training and experience to fill the position.

I graduate from Martin Luther King, Jr., High School June 16, 1989, and will be ready for employment any time after that date.

In high school I had perfect attendance and maintained a B average grade. In my senior year, I participated in our school's Office Education Training Program.

Through this special program, I acquired on-the-job experience as an assistant sales correspondent for the Value Insurance Company. My duties included taking dictation, transcribing, handling routine correspondence, and managing the appointment book for six sales representatives. In this position, I discovered an aptitude and a liking for writing that I hope to develop in business.

I participated in many extracurricular activities. The most challenging was a successful campaign to raise $2000 for the Future Business Leaders of America Club.

I will be happy to supply references to you upon request.

I can be reached at 415-777-7777 after 4:30 p.m.

Dear Mr. Sebastian:

The position you advertised in the October 7 *Record* is exactly the opportunity I had hoped to find. As I read the ad, I felt that you were talking to me.

As the enclosed résumé shows, I will graduate from SUNY in early June with a major in marketing. I feel that I have an excellent marketing education (18 semester hours), supported by a broad program in general business. Of special interest to me was my work in marketing research, in which I received high honors.

I would like very much to meet you and tell you in person why I believe I can be useful to your organization. I have a strong interest in marketing research, and I am eager to learn from the specialists in your company more about this exciting field.

I am usually home by 4 p.m. (555-1234) each weekday except Wednesday, when I play tennis.

FISHING LETTER

The fishing letter is written to companies that you select. It does not respond to a particular ad, so it must be more thorough. Since the company has not advertised for a particular position, you need to tell the reader more about yourself and your reasons for writing. The advantages of a fishing letter are that it tells the company you have had the initiative to look them up and, more, that you like what you saw and want to work for them.

Although possibly flattered by your interest, the recipient of your fishing letter must quickly be given reason to read on. You must give a detailed description of your skills and show how they relate to this company to interest the person in reading further and going on to your résumé.

The importance of tailoring your approach to the particular company is even more crucial than in a cover letter. You want to show the reader that you are especially suited to the needs of the company. (See Chapter 2 for more tips on the fishing letter.)

Dear Ms. Philbrook:

I am writing to ask about the possibility of employment with Long, North & Greenhouse as an acquisitions editor.

Since 1983 I have worked for Pirin Books New York, advancing to the position of senior acquisitions editor for biology and chemistry. In July of 1985, I transferred to the Heidelberg, West Germany, headquarters office. For personal reasons, however, I have recently returned to the United States. I am therefore currently looking for new opportunities to continue my publishing career here.

While at Pirin Books, I developed a publishing program in biology, chemistry, and the basic biomedical sciences that now consists of more than 100 books, book series, and journals. I also managed a large program of titles imported from the parent company, making the primary recommendation on the North American price and print run and dealing with the marketing for these titles.

I have always admired Long, North & Greenhouse's approach to publishing. I believe that with my experience I can make a significant contribution to a company such as yours. Should my qualifications be of interest, I would welcome meeting with you.

Dear Mr. Murphy:

This letter is an application for a position in merchandising with your company. I have just graduated from Wesleyan University with a degree in Business Administration, and I am eager to begin working—especially with an organization such as yours.

The enclosed résumé gives all the pertinent facts about my education and employment history. I am particularly interested in working for the L&M Corporation because the department store field has always appealed to me. All the part-time positions I held while in school were in this field.

I would be happy to accept any position in the field of merchandising. I want to learn all phases of this work. My main interest is to work with an organization such as yours, where I believe I would receive excellent training.

I would appreciate a personal interview with you to enable me to convince you of my enthusiasm and sincerity. May I call you on the telephone Wednesday, October 7, at 11 a.m. for an appointment?

Thank you for your interest.

Dear Mr. Watanabe:

Do you have a place in the Accounting Department at Lundgren Oil for a young man who:

1. Hopes to make a career in accounting, specifically in the petroleum industry?

2. Has an educational background in accounting, including courses in petroleum accounting?

3. Is eager to learn and not afraid to dig in?

On June 10 I graduate from State University, and I am eager to find a challenging position in the Portland area.

A complete description of my qualifications is enclosed. Would you let me know, please, whether you have a place in your organization for me? Thank you!

REFERENCE REQUEST LETTER

If you plan to put someone's name, address, and phone number at the bottom of your résumé, you *must* get that person's permission before you do so. Write a brief letter explaining what you plan to do, why you want to use his or her name, and a sincere request for approval. Since your reference will be getting calls about you, which is rather an imposition, it is important that you show that you understand what you are asking for.

There are three major categories of people whom you will ask to use as references. These categories may overlap. They are:

1. Someone familiar with your educational background—professor or teacher, dean, principal, or other school employee

2. Former employers

3. Someone who can vouch for your general character, such as a rabbi or priest, a friend who has established a good reputation locally (perhaps one who owns a business), or a prominent citizen who knows you personally

Dear Judge Young,

Graduation is only a months away, and if all goes well, I will receive my BBA degree from the University of Atlanta. I don't know who will be happier—me or my dad!

I am preparing to look for a job. My interest is in marketing research, and I hope to find a management trainee position in a large company not too far away. May I use your name as a reference? If you are willing to vouch for me, just write "OK" at the bottom of this letter and return it in the enclosed stamped and addressed envelope.

Best wishes to you and Mrs. Young. I will be in Gainesville about June 8, and I hope to see both of you then.

Dear Ms. Cortes,

I will be applying for a position as an accountant in the St. Louis area in the coming weeks, and I would like to use your name as a reference.

Since you always spoke highly of my ability with figures and accounting when I was in your class, I feel comfortable asking you to vouch for me. As a professor at a business school, your support will be particularly helpful for me.

If I may put your name and telephone number on my résumé, please just initial the enclosed card and return it in the stamped, addressed envelope I have included. I very much appreciate your help.

Dear Elizabeth,

It has been a pleasure working under you the past 2 years. I have appreciated your honesty, guidance, and encouragement as supervisor.

I am sorry to leave Twiller Corporation, but, as you know, I am moving out of the area and cannot continue my work here.

I would be grateful to you if you would permit me to use your name as a reference on my résumé. I would not ask this if I did not feel that you had approved of my work at Twiller while I was reporting to you.

If this will be acceptable to you, you can reach me at the above address and phone. I am usually home between 3 and 7 p.m. Thank you in advance for your assistance.

FOLLOW-UP LETTER

After a job interview, immediately write a short note to the person who interviewed you. The main purpose of this note is to keep your name "active" during the selection process.

In it, thank the interviewer for taking the time to talk with you about the job and your career interests. You might restate any important point that was made, or you might say that the interview reinforced your positive feelings about the job.

Keep it brief and to the point. You want to remind the interviewer of your name and impress upon him or her your enthusiasm, but remember your reader is very busy, and you don't want to seem too pushy. (For more on follow-up letters, see Chapter 2.)

Dear Mr. Ahmad:

Thank you for the opportunity to discuss your management training opening last Thursday. After meeting with you and your staff I am very excited about the possibility of working for Ellisworth Enterprises. It seems exactly the sort of challenging, educational opportunity I had hoped to find.

I look forward to hearing from you again.

Dear Ms. Crevel:

Thank you for the chance to talk to you about my qualifications for the vacancy in your travel agency. I appreciated meeting your general manager, Mr. Alfred Tulare. Now I know why Round Trip Tours is number 1 in the nation in wholesale travel sales.

This experience has made me even more eager to work with all of you. I look forward to hearing from you about the job.

Dear Mr. Lockwood:

Thank you for a pleasant meeting this week to discuss the position as your executive assistant. I enjoyed becoming acquainted with you.

The job is very attractive to me; I know I would find the work challenging and satisfying.

After learning more about the duties, I realize that my knowledge of advanced statistical methods may be light. The subject intrigues me, however, and I really want to learn more about it. I did well in the one course on statistics I completed at Mitchell College. I notice that Mohonk Valley College offers advanced programs in statistics, and I would enroll for this training in the evening division.

Please express my appreciation to Mr. Cullen and Ms. Roh for giving me so much of their time.

Decisions can take a long time. This is especially true if the job is an important one and there are a lot of applicants. Most companies notify applicants when a decision has been made, but some do not. If you have not heard anything after a week or two, write another brief letter asking for information.

Writing to ask for this information, reiterating your interest in the job, can bring up your name again at the point when a decision is about to be made, and it may favorably affect the outcome. At the very least, it will get you the information that a decision has been made and you are not the lucky one. That is better than wondering about what happened for the next few weeks.

Continue to maintain a positive tone in your letter:

- Don't sound impatient.

- Don't assume that you ought to have been chosen.

- Don't demand that you be informed of their decision.

Simply state your interest in the job, and inquire politely whether a decision has been made. You may be impatient, nervous, even crabby, but don't show it!

Dear Mr. Sukarno:

You were kind enough to speak with me on August 18 about

the position of appointments secretary for which you were then seeking applicants.

I wanted to write and confirm my interest in the position. I am still eager to begin working. I feel that I have the right skills and aptitudes to succeed and to make a contribution to your firm.

I look forward to hearing from you as soon as a decision has been made.

ACCEPTING A JOB OFFER

Accepting a job is one of the nicest letters you will ever write. But don't let it fool you; it still requires your attention and the use of the skills you have learned from the more difficult correspondence. It remains important to present an image of intelligence, organization, courtesy, and cooperation. Think of this as your first official act as a new employee.

Other letters need to be written at this time as well. You will want to thank the people whose names you used as references on your résumé (see material on thank-you notes in Chapter 9), and you will want to inform anyone else who has considered you for a job that you are no longer to be considered an applicant (see below, "Declining a Job Offer").

In writing the acceptance letter, let your natural enthusiasm show. Be positive, and thank the person who has been the bearer of good tidings. It is a natural reaction to feel grateful; let this come out in your letter. Say that you look forward to the job. Again, since the essence of the letter is simple, keep it short and right to the point; don't go overboard. A few lines are all that is necessary. Be sure to acknowledge the time when you are to report to work.

Dear Mr. Upton:

I am delighted to accept the position in the research department at Universal Corporation. I will report to the medical office at 9 a.m. on October 8 for a physical examination and will go directly to your office afterward, as you suggested.

The prospect of joining your team is very exciting. I look forward to getting started. I will read the material you sent me with much interest.

Dear Ms. Alieri:

Thank you so much for your telephone call telling me I have been chosen for the word processor position at Crowell Systems. I am naturally delighted and look forward to demonstrating that your confidence in me has not been misplaced.

I will report to the office for my orientation period on Monday, July 15, as you requested. I am looking forward to starting work. Thanks again!

DECLINING A JOB OFFER

This is a short, to-the-point letter that states its message simply and clearly without trying to justify or explain. If you feel particularly friendly toward the reader or the company, you might want to mention that, or say that your reasons for declining the job do not reflect negatively on them.

Avoid saying negative things about the job you are declining. You never know; you may end up looking for work with them again in the future, and you don't want to say anything that might jeopardize your chances.

If you do not feel particularly friendly toward the company (if, for example, you have an application in and have not heard from them in some time), simply write that you have had a better offer (or whatever your reason may be) and are no longer to be considered an applicant. Close with a brief word of thanks for whatever consideration you may have received.

To a company that has not followed up the interview:

Dear Mr. Ahmad:

This is to let you know that I have accepted a research position with another company. Therefore, I am no longer an applicant for the job I applied for in your organization.

I appreciate whatever consideration you gave my application.

To a company that has shown interest:

Dear Ms. Mabuto:

Thank you very much for offering me the position of research assistant at Uptown Research Concerns.

Shortly after I applied to Uptown, I was encouraged to apply to fill a vacancy in the Research and Development Department in a large company near Olympia. I did so and was notified yesterday that I had been selected. I immediately accepted the offer.

I am grateful for the opportunity you offered and appreciate your confidence in me.

SUMMING UP

Try to be as businesslike as possible whenever you write for a job. Compare your letter to the way you would dress for a job interview. You would take every effort to be neat, not flashy, to give an impression of seriousness and reliability. Do the same for your words. Present yourself in as organized and efficient a manner as possible.

Résumés require the same attitude. The résumé is a glorified list—stick to that idea and you won't go far wrong. Watch out for getting too wordy in your descriptions of what you've done. A lot of that can be covered in the interview. Start by writing down everything you can think of, then number your experiences and skills according to their importance and relevance to your career goal or the job you are seeking.

Don't forget to keep in touch! Let that employer know you're out there, eager to go to work. Thank him or her for the time taken for your interview, and if you don't hear anything for a couple of weeks, write and ask what your status is. Don't be pushy and don't be cute—just make your request. They'll remember you, and they might even get to like your persistence. Good luck.

A FINAL WORD

Words are the soul's ambassadors, who go
Abroad upon her errands to and fro;
They are the sole expounders of the mind,
And correspondence keep 'twixt all mankind.

—James Howell (1595?–1666)

USEFUL REFERENCE
WORKS

In many books on writing, you will find a long list of recommended reference books to use after you've finished the one you are reading, which strikes us as not particularly helpful. Who has time to look through them all? What we provide here is a representative list of the best available books covering different aspects of good writing, from putting together a résumé to how to construct a sentence, should you want to delve deeper into the art of writing.

In addition to what is listed below, don't forget the dictionary! A good unabridged dictionary is an absolutely indispensable tool for any writer, whether professional or occasional. For spelling, usage, and the subtle connotations that flavor a piece of writing—not to mention the everyday definitions—the dictionary provides a wealth of information that is unavailable anywhere else.

Bolles, Richard Nelson, *What Color is Your Parachute? A Practical Manual for Job-Hunters and Career-Changers,* Ten Speed Press, Berkeley, Calif., 1982 (for résumés and other job-related material).
Chicago Manual of Style, University of Chicago, 13th ed, Chicago/London, 1982.
Hutchinson, Lois Irene, *Standard Handbook for Secretaries,* 8th ed, McGraw-Hill, New York, 1969.

Perrin, Porter G., *Writer's Guide and Index to English,* 5th ed, Scott, Foresman, Glenview, Ill., 1972.

Sabin, William A., *The Gregg Reference Manual,* 6th ed, McGraw-Hill, New York, 1985.

Strunk, William, Jr., and E. B. White, *The Elements of Style,* 2d ed, MacMillan, New York, 1972.

Todd, Alden, *Finding Facts Fast: How to Find Out What You Want and Need to Know,* 2d ed, Ten Speed Press, Berkeley, Calif., 1979.

U.S. Government Printing Office Style Manual, rev. ed., U.S. Government Printing Office, Washington, D.C. 1973.

INDEX

Abbreviations:
   in dates, 91
   in memos, 155
   in return addresses, 88
Acceptances:
   of invitations, 190–191
   of job offers, 246–247
   of speaking invitations, 131–132
Active voice, 14–15, 30
Addresses:
   interior, in letters, 91–92
   return, on letters, 85–89
Advice, 74
Advise, 75
Affect, 75
All ready, 75
All right and *alright*, 75
Already, 75
Anger, 48–49
Apostrophe ('), 70–71
Appraise, 76
Apprise, 76
Asterisk (*), 71
Attention lines in business letters, 93

Babies, births of: congratulatory
      letters for, 186
   thank-you letters for gifts for, 188
Bad, 76
Badly, 76

bc or *bcc* (blind copy), 108
   of memos, 147
Bibliographies in reports, 175
Bills:
   for credit cards, letters regarding,
      201–203
   letters on inability to pay, 44, 201
   letters seeking payment of, 135–137
Birthdays, thank-you letters for gifts
      for, 187
Births of babies:
   congratulatory letters for, 186
   thank-you letters for gifts for, 188
Blind copies:
   of letters, 108
   of memos, 147
Block-style letters, 109–110
Blowing-off-steam letters, 40–42, 205,
      207
Bodies of reports, 170–172
Books on writing, 250–251
Brevity, 15–18
   in active voice, 14
Business letters:
   accepting job offers, 246–247
   agreeing to something in, 131–132
   asking for something in, 128–131
   attention lines in, 93
   complimentary close omitted from,
      101–102

Business letters (*Cont.*):
copy notations in, 107–108
cover, with résumés, 35–36, 237–240
dates on, 117–118
declining job offers, 247–248
declining something, 132–133
enclosures with, 106–107
"fishing" (seeking employment),
44–46, 240–242
following-up on interviews, 47–48,
244–246
formats for, 109–114
interior addresses in, 92
of introduction, 126–127, 191–192
letterheads for, 89
making and confirming reservations,
127–128
memos distinguished from, 143
offering credit, 133–134
offering a job, 137–139
ordering merchandise, 208–209
within personal letters, 181
providing information, 118–120
reference initials in, 106
references, 192–195
refusing credit, 134–135
rejecting a job applicant, 139–140
requesting credit, 198–200
requesting references, 242–243
of resignation, 140–142
sales, 32–35, 122–126
salutations omitted in, 94
salutations used in, 95–96
seeking information, 120–122,
203–204
seeking payment, 135–137
subject lines in, 100–101
(*See also* Employment; Letters;
Memos; Résumés)
Business reports (*see* Reports)
Business titles, 92
at end of letters, 106

c (copy), 108
Capital, 76
Capital letters:
for emphasis, 55–56
in subject lines, in business letters,
100–101
Capitol, 76

Carroll, Lewis, 12
cc (carbon copy), 108, 147
Christmas cards, 79
Clarity, 19–21
Clauses:
restrictive and nonrestrictive, 69
semicolons to separate, 67
Closes in letters, 101–105
Closing paragraphs, 63
College application essays, 216–219
Colon (:), 67–68
in salutations, 94
Comma (,), 68–70
anxiety about, 66
inside quotation marks, 73
in return addresses, 88
in salutations, 94
Commercials, 2
Committees, reports as results of,
165–166
Communal letters, 183–185
Communications:
memos for, 143
writing for, 7, 179
Company names in salutations, 98
Complaint letters, 40–42, 204–207
closing paragraphs in, 63
copy notations on, 107
regarding credit cards, 202–203
Complimentary closings in letters,
101–105
Complimentary letters, 107–108
Compliments in memos, 158–160
Compose, 77
Compound words, 71–72
Comprise, 77
Computers, 80, 115, 168
(*See also* Word processors)
Conclusions for reports, 172
Conditional statements, 54
Condolence letters, 26–27, 195–196
handwritten, 80
"Confidential" on envelopes, 93
Confirmations of reservations, 128
Congratulatory letters, 25–26,
185–186
handwritten, 80
Congress, letters to, 209–212
Conjunctions not used with
semicolons, 67

Contents, tables of, in reports,
174–175
Contractions, apostrophes for, 70
Copies:
communal letters as, 183–185
of memos, etiquette of, 146–147
notations of, on business letters,
107–108
Correction fluids, 80
Couples, salutations for, 99–100
Courtesy titles, 91–92
at end of letters, 106
Cover letters for résumés, 35–36,
237–240
Credit:
letters denying, 43–44, 134–135
letters offering, 133–134
letters requesting, 198–200
Credit card letters, 201–203
"CYA syndrome," 144

Dash (—), 56, 67
Dates:
on business letters, 117–118
on letters, 89–91
of meetings, in memos, 155–156
Day-of-the-week, 90
Dear, 93–97
Dear Sir, 121
Declinations:
of invitations, 190–191
of job offers, 247–248
of speaking invitations, 132–133
Direct mail, 122
Directions, information in, 18
Double salutations, 98–100

Editors, letters to, 212–216
Education:
college application essays for,
216–219
on résumés, 225
Effect, 75
Emphasis:
in sentences, 54–55
underlining and capitals for, 55–56
Employment:
congratulatory letters for promotions
in, 185–186
"fishing" letters for, 44–46, 240–242

Employment (*Cont.*):
letters accepting offers of, 246–247
letters declining offers of, 247–248
letters offering, 137–139
letters rejecting applicants for,
139–140
memos recommending promotions,
160–161
reference letters for, 192–195
reference request letters for,
242–243
resignation letters from, 140–142
résumé cover letters for, 35–36,
237–240
résumés for, 223–237
thank-you letters following
interviews for, 47–48, 244–246
warning memos regarding, 153–154
writing for, 223
(*See also* Business letters)
Enclosures with business letters,
106–107
Engagements, congratulatory letters
for, 186
Envelopes marked "personal" or
"confidential," 93
Errors:
in credit card accounts, letters
regarding, 201–203
in handwritten letters, 80
Essays in college applications, 216–219
Etiquette:
of sending copies of memos,
146–147
of thank-you letters for wedding
gifts, 187
European date format, 90–91
Exclamation point (!), 56, 66–67
inside quotation and, 73
in salutations, 94
Executive summaries in reports, 168,
172–173
Experience:
in college application essays,
218–219
on résumés, 224–225

Faking interest, 12–13
Family, communal letters to, 183–185
Favors, thank-you letters for, 188

Federal government agencies,
    information requested from, 212
File cards in note taking, 167–168
Finalize, 120
First paragraphs, 61–63
"Fishing" letters (seeking
    employment), 44–46, 240–242
Formats:
    for business letters, 109–114
    for dates, 90–91
    for letters to editors, 214
    for memos, 144–146
    for reports, 166, 170–171
    for résumés, 224
Full-pause punctuation, 66–67
FYI (for your information), 148

Gentlemen, 98
Gifts, thank-you letters for, 187–188
Good, 77
Government agencies, requests for
    information from, 212
Grammar, 50–51
    active and passive voice in, 14–15
    common errors of, 78–79
Greeting cards, 79, 80
Greetings, 97

Habits in writing:
    bad, 8–13
    good, 13–22
Half-pause punctuation, 67–68
Hazlitt, William, 19
Headings:
    in memos, 144–146
    in reports, 166, 169
Hedging, 8–10, 29–30
    passive voice in, 14
Howell, James, 249
Humor, 48–49
Hyphen (-), 71–72

I, 35–40
    me versus, 79
    in memos, 149–150
Imply, 77
Infer, 77
Information:
    completeness of, 18
    from congresspersons, 211–212

Information (*Cont.*):
    letters providing, 118–120
    letters seeking, 120–122, 203–204
    letters sharing, 36–38
    memos seeking, 152–153
    memos sharing, 147–151
Initials, reference, in business letters,
    106
Inks, 80
Instructions:
    information in, 18–19
    memos giving, 156–158
    parallel construction in, 53–54
    style for, 27–32
Intensives, 56
Interior addresses in letters, 91–92
Interviews:
    in research, 167
    thank-you letters following, 47–48,
    244–246
Introduction, letters of, 126–127,
    191–192
Introductions in reports, 169–170
Invitations, 188–190
    letters accepting or declining,
    190–191
    to speak, 129–130
Its and *it's,* 70–71

Jobs (*see* Employment)

Laird, Charlton, 67
Last paragraphs, 63
Legibility, 79–80
Length:
    of letters to editors, 214
    of sentences, 53
    of words, 11–12
Letterheads, 85–89
Letters:
    accepting or declining invitations,
    190–191
    accepting job offers, 246–247
    agreeing to something, 131–132
    asking for something, 128–131
    attention lines on, 93
    bodies of, 101
    business, formats for, 109–114
    colons in salutations in, 67–68
    commas in salutations in, 70

Letters (*Cont.*):
  communal, 183–185
  complaint, 40–42, 204–207
  complimentary, 107–108
  complimentary closes in, 101–105
  compliments in, 158
  condolence, 26–27, 195–196
  congratulatory, 25–26, 185–186
  to Congress, 209–212
  copy notations on, 107–108
  cover, for résumés, 35–36, 237–240
  dates on, 89–91, 117–118
  declining job offers, 247–248
  declining something, 132–133
  to the editor, 212–216
  enclosures with, 106–107
  "fishing" (seeking employment),
    44–46, 240–242
  following-up on interviews, 47–48,
    244–246
  handwritten, 80
  humor, sarcasm, and anger in, 48–49
  on inability to pay bills, 44, 201
  interior addresses on, 91–92
  of introduction, 126–127, 191–192
  invitations, 188–190
  making and confirming reservations,
    127–128
  memos distinguished from, 143
  names and signatures on, 105–106
  names used in salutations in, 39
  names used in text of, 40
  with negative messages, 42–44
  offering credit, 133–134
  offering a job, 137–139
  order of paragraphs in, 62–63
  ordering merchandise, 208–209
  personal, 79, 179–183, 196–197
  postscripts on, 108–109
  providing information, 118–120
  of reference, 192–195
  reference initials in, 106
  refusing credit, 43–44, 134–135
  regarding credit cards, 201–203
  rejecting a job applicant, 139–140
  requesting credit, 198–200
  requesting references, 242–243
  of resignation, 140–142
  return addresses and letterheads for,
    85–89

Letters (*Cont.*):
  sales, 32–35, 122–126
  salutations in, 93–100
  seeking information, 120–122,
    203–204
  seeking payment, 135–137
  sharing information, 36–38
  subject lines in, 100–101
  thank-you, 47–48, 186–188
  (*See also* Business letters; Personal
    letters)
Lists:
  numbered, in letters, 121–122
  parentheses used in, 72

Magazines, letters to editors of,
    212–216
Maiden names in salutations, 100
Mail order merchandise, 208–209
Married couples, salutations for,
    99–100
Me, I versus, 79
Meetings:
  memos setting up, 154–156
  memos summarizing actions at,
    151
  minutes of, 220–222
Memos, 143, 163–164
  etiquette of sending copies of,
    146–147
  extending compliments, 158–160
  giving instructions, 27–32, 156–158
  headings on, 144–146
  paragraph structure in, 57–58
  recommending promotions, 160–161
  requesting action, 161–163
  scheduling meetings, 154–156
  seeking information, 152–153
  sharing information, 147–152
  transitional words and phrases in,
    59–61
  warning, 153–154
Merchandise orders, 208–209
Messrs. (Messieurs), 95
Middle paragraphs, 63
Middle sentences, 57
Minutes of meetings, 151, 220–222
Miss, 95
Modified-block-style letters, 111
  with indented paragraphs, 112

Modifiers:
compound, hyphens in, 72
word order of, 52
Montaigne, Michel Eyquem de, 4
Mr., 106
Ms., 95

Names:
in interior addresses, in letters, 92
possessive forms of, 71
in salutations, 39, 94, 97
signatures and, 105–106
used in text of letters, 40
Negative messages, 42–44
Negative tone in complaint letters, 41
Negatives in parallel construction, 53
Newspapers, letters to editors of,
212–216
Nicknames in salutations, 97
Nonrestrictive clauses, 69
Nonverbal communications, 1
Not, 21
Notes in report writing, 167–168
Numbered lists in letters, 121–122
Numbers, 73
in dates, 91

Observing in research, 167
Opinion letters:
to Congress, 209–212
to editors, 212–216
Order of words, 51–52
Ordering merchandise, 208–209
Outlines, 166

Paragraphs:
first and last, 61–63
structure of, 56–58
transitions in, 59–61
Parallel construction, 26, 28, 38, 42,
53–54
Parentheses [()], 72–73
Passive voice, 14–15
in hedging, 10
Payments, letters seeking, 135–137
Pencils, 80
Pens, 80
Period (.), 66
inside quotation marks, 73
"Personal" on envelopes, 93

Personal letters, 179–183, 196–197
accepting or declining invitations,
190–191
accepting job offers, 246–247
for action, 198, 222
communal, 183–185
of complaint, 204–207
complimentary closings in, 103–105
condolence, 26–27, 195–196
congratulatory, 25–26, 185–186
to Congress, 209–212
dates on, 90
declining job offers, 247–248
to the editor, 212–216
on inability to pay bills, 44, 201
interior addresses in, 92
of introduction, 191–192
invitations, 188–190
legibility of, 79
ordering merchandise, 208–209
to organizations, 93
of reference, 192–195
regarding credit cards, 201–203
requesting credit, 198–200
return addresses on, 86
salutations in, 96–97
seeking information, 203–204
thank you, 47–48, 186–188
(*See also* Letters)
Personal pronouns, 35–40
Phrases, transitional, 59–61
Plurals, apostrophes not used to form,
71
Pompous words, 11–12
Pope, Alexander, 81
Positive wording, 21–22
in complaint letters, 41
in memos, 60–61
in negative messages, 42–44
in sales letters, 33
Possessive pronouns, apostrophes not
used with, 71
Possessives, apostrophes for, 70–71
Postscripts, 108–109
PPS (post-postscript), 109
Principal, 77–78
Principle, 78
Professional titles, 91–92
at end of letters, 105
in salutations, 95

Promotions:
    congratulatory letters for, 185–186
    memos recommending, 160–161
Pronouns:
    apostrophes not used with, 71
    we, 149–150
    you and *I,* 32, 35–40, 79, 213
PS (postscript), 109
Punctuation, 65–66
    apostrophes, 70–71
    full-pause, 66–67
    half-pause, 67–68
    miscellaneous, 71–73
    of salutations, 94
    slight-pause, 68–70
Punctuation marks, 66, 71–73
    in return addresses, 88

Question mark (?), 66–67
    inside quotation and, 73
Quotation marks (" "), 73

Reading:
    average speed of, 2
    in research, 167
Recommendations:
    letters requesting, 242–243
    reference letters for, 192–195
    in reports, 172
Redundant words, 11
Reference initials in business letters,
    106
Reference works, 250–251
References:
    for credit, 199
    letters of, 192–195
    letters requesting, 242–243
    on résumés, 226
Reports, 165–166, 176
    bodies of, 170–172
    conclusions to, 172
    executive summaries to, 172–173
    introductions to, 169–170
    notes for, 167–168
    optional elements of, 173–175
    outlines for, 166
    research for, 166–167
Research for reports, 166–167
Reservations, letters to make and to
    confirm, 127–128

Resignation letters, 140–142
Restrictive clauses, 69
Résumés, 223–224, 248
    content of, 224–226
    cover letters for, 35–36, 237–240
    "fishing" letters and, 44–46, 240–242
    pointers for writing, 226–227
    preparation and organization of,
        227–228
    reference request letters and,
        242–243
    samples of, 228–237
Return addresses on letters, 85–89

Sales letters, 32–35, 122–126
    letters of introduction as, 126–127
Salutations, 93–100
    colons in, 67–68
    commas in, 70
    Dear Sir, 121
    names used in, 39
    in sales letters, 33
Sarcasm, 48–49
Semicolon (;), 67
Senate, letters to, 209–212
Sentences:
    commas in, 68–70
    different structures used in, 38
    emphasis in, 54–56
    length of, 53
    numbers used in, 73
    in paragraphs, 56–58
    parallel construction in, 26, 28,
        53–54
    punctuation to end, 66–67
    word order in, 51–52
Sexist usage in salutations, 98, 121
Signatures, 105–106
    printed, on greeting cards, 79
Simplified-style letters, 113–114
Slight-pause punctuation, 68–70
Southbey, Robert, 15
Spaces between words, 65
Speeches and talks:
    invitations to give, 129–130
    letters agreeing to give, 131–132
    letters declining to give, 132–133
Spelling, 74–78
    grammar and, 78–79
Stafford, Kim, 53

State names, abbreviations for, 88
Strunk, William, Jr., 14
Style, 24
  for business letters, 109–114
  caring tone in, 25–26
  of complaint letters, 40–42
  of "fishing" letters (seeking
      employment), 44–46
  in giving instructions, 27–32
  humor, sarcasm and anger in, 48–49
  for interior addresses, in letters, 92
  of negative messages, 42–44
  of reference letters, 193–195
  for return addresses, 88
  in sales letters, 32–35
  of thank-you letters, 47–48
  tone in, 26–27
  you and *I* in, 35–40
Subject lines:
  in business letters, 100–101
  in memo headings, 146
Summary sentences, 57
Superlatives, 12
Sympathy notes, 26–27, 195–196
  handwritten, 80

Tables of contents for reports, 174–175
Telephone, 179, 180
  to respond to invitations, 190
Telephone numbers on letterheads, 85
Thank you in memos, 162
Thank-you letters, 186–188
  following interviews, 47–48
That, 69
Their, 78
There, 78
Title pages for reports, 174
Titles:
  at end of letters, 105–106
  in interior addresses, in letters,
      91–92
  in memo headings, 146
  in salutations, 94–95, 98, 99
  underlining and quotation marks for,
      73
TO (in memos), 144
To Whom It May Concern, 98
Todd, Alden, 167
Tone, 26–27
  caring, 25–26

Topic sentences, 57
Transitions in paragraphs,
    59–61
Twain, Mark, 21
Typewriters, 80
Typists, reference initials for,
    106

Underlining, 56
  for titles, 73
Unique, 79
Unmarried couples, salutations for,
    100

Vagueness, 22
Verbal communications, 1

Warning memos, 153–154
We, 149–150
Wedding gifts, thank-you letters for,
    187
Well, 77
Which, 69
White, E. B., 14
Women:
  excluded from *Dear Sir* salutation,
      121
  requests for credit by, 199, 200
  salutations for, 95
Word processors:
  creating executive summaries using,
      173
  dates on letters inserted by,
      118
  for résumé preparation, 227
  tables of contents generated by,
      174–175
Words:
  clarity of, 19–21
  order of, 51–52
  pompous, 11–12
  positive and specific, 21–22
  quotations marks around, 73
  spaces between, 65
  superlatives, 12
  transitional, 59–61
  underlining and capitals for,
      55–56
  using too many, 10–11
Work (*see* Employment)

Writing:
  bad habits in, 8–13
  books on, 250–251
  in communications, 179
  good habits in, 13–22
  grammar in, 50–51
  legibility of, 79–80
  for pleasure, 179–180

Writing (*Cont.*):
  receivers of, 7–8
  as verbal communications, 1

You, 35–40
  in letters to editors, 213
  as understood subject, 32
Yours and *your's,* 71